T0318620

Quantum Service-oriented Computing: A Proposal for Quantum Software as a Service

Published 2024 by River Publishers

River Publishers

Alsbjergvej 10, 9260 Gistrup, Denmark

www.riverpublishers.com

Distributed exclusively by Routledge

605 Third Avenue, New York, NY 10017, USA

4 Park Square, Milton Park, Abingdon, Oxon OX14 4RN

Quantum Service-oriented Computing: A Proposal for Quantum Software as a Service / by Javier Romero-Álvarez, Jaime Alvarado-Valiente, Enrique Moguel, José Garcia-Alonso, Juan M. Murillo.

Routledge is an imprint of the Taylor & Francis Group, an informa business

ISBN 978-87-7004-199-7 (paperback)

ISBN 978-87-7004-642-8 (online)

ISBN 978-87-7004-633-6 (ebook master)

A Publication in the River Publishers Series in Rapids

While every effort is made to provide dependable information, the publisher, authors, and editors cannot be held responsible for any errors or omissions.

Quantum Service-oriented Computing: A Proposal for Quantum Software as a Service

Javier Romero-Álvarez

Universidad de Extremadura, Spain

Jaime Alvarado-Valiente

Universidad de Extremadura, Spain

Enrique Moguel

Universidad de Extremadura, Spain

José Garcia-Alonso

Universidad de Extremadura, Spain

Juan M. Murillo

Universidad de Extremadura, Spain

Routledge
Taylor & Francis Group

NEW YORK AND LONDON

Contents

Prologue

All computer experts agree that this decade is "the" quantum decade and that we can already take advantage of quantum computers, which have demonstrated a transformative potential in computational capabilities, presenting a paradigm shift in information processing. Quantum computers take advantage of the principles of superposition and entanglement, allowing them to process multiple possibilities "simultaneously," thus solving certain problems (e.g. optimization and simulation) much more efficiently. In fact, completely new solutions are possible in multiple business areas: economics and financial services, chemistry, medicine and healthcare, supply chain and logistics, energy, agriculture, etc.

In any case, we must be aware that the key lies in the integration of classical and quantum technologies since quantum computing does not replace traditional computing. We will increasingly witness the existence of hybrid systems (quantum/classical) in which each of the technologies will be used for what it is best suited for.

As we insisted in The Talavera Manifesto for Quantum Software Engineering and Programming, of which the authors of the book are among the main drivers, we believe that the time has come to address the production of quantum software and systems by applying the knowledge and lessons learned in this field. This involves applying or adapting existing processes, methods, techniques, practices, and engineering principles to the development of quantum software and services.

Service-oriented architectures (SOAs) can play a pivotal role in addressing the unique challenges posed by quantum computing and hybrid systems. SOAs provide a flexible and modular framework, enabling the seamless integration of quantum computing services into existing computational ecosystems. This adaptability is crucial as quantum technologies evolve, ensuring compatibility with diverse applications and facilitating the incorporation of quantum algorithms into existing workflows.

Additionally, SOAs allow for efficient resource allocation, scalability, and abstraction, empowering users to leverage quantum capabilities without delving deeply into the intricacies of quantum hardware. The adoption of SOAs thus becomes imperative for unlocking the full potential of quantum computing across various domains of scientific research and the business world.

This book provides an overview of how these revolutionary concepts are beginning to be integrated into the development and deployment of web services, heralding a profound transformation of the technology industry. This book proposes a scenario in which quantum services not only offer greater processing power and efficiency but also promote greater integration and synergy between different technologies and platforms.

To facilitate the understanding of all concepts, the content of this book is logically structured from a perspective of web engineering for quantum services, providing a new vision for any reader and both for those who wish to enter the world of quantum computing, as well as in preparation for its development and application from the prism of service orientation.

In the field of quantum research, the authors of this book (long-time internationally recognized experts in the field of web services) devote considerable effort to the advancement of quantum engineering. Their research efforts aim to push the boundaries and contribute to the evolution of quantum computing and its practical applications, with a special focus on software engineering. With this book, the authors invite readers to explore the landscape of quantum computing and the derived aspects of quantum services.

In summary, I consider this a great work where the knowledge and R&D work of the authors in the field of service-oriented quantum computing is reflected and, from my point of view, will contribute to its dissemination and to the stimulation of many professionals to get into these technologies and adopt them in their professional activity.

Congratulations to the authors on producing this valuable and timely book on quantum web service engineering!

Prof. Mario Piattini

Ciudad Real, Spain

January 2024

Preface

The field of quantum computing has been rapidly evolving in recent years, with the potential to revolutionize the way we approach complex problems in several fields. As such, there is a growing need for a comprehensive guide that covers the foundational principles of quantum computing, as well as its practical applications in the development of quantum services.

The purpose of this book is to provide a comprehensive exploration of quantum computing, covering from its foundational principles to its practical applications in the development of quantum services. It begins with a review of the fundamental aspects of quantum computing, explaining concepts such as qubits, superposition, and entanglement, targeting readers with varying degrees of familiarity with the subject.

Beyond the basic concepts, the book goes on to explore some of the challenges faced by quantum software developers in the current landscape. To this end, it addresses issues related to low-level abstractions and the absence of integration, deployment, and quality assurance mechanisms in quantum software engineering.

In addition, it explores the principles of Service-Oriented Computing (SOC) applied to quantum computing, revealing architectural patterns tailored for quantum computing and discussing standardization and accessibility in this field.

The book also provides a vision for future directions in the evolving landscape of Quantum Computing as a Service.

With all this, we can define the main purposes pursued by this book:

- Establish an understanding of quantum computing, from its basic concepts to its application in the development of quantum services.
- Provide a detailed overview of the current challenges faced by quantum software developers.

- Explore the landscape of quantum computing and the derived aspects of quantum services.
- Explore the principles learned from SOC applied to quantum computing.
- Analyze architectural and adaptive patterns for quantum computing.
- Address standardization and accessibility, discussing the role of standardization tools and continuous deployment in the generation and deployment of quantum services.
- Provide the reader an analysis of the future of quantum computing and the main conclusions drawn from the work done by the community up to the present day.

Content

To address the above objectives, the book is organized in the following chapters:

Chapter 1 lays the foundation for the book, introducing the motivation behind quantum computing and providing a comprehensive overview of key concepts. Fundamental principles such as qubits, superposition, entanglement, and most important quantum algorithms are explored. The chapter also delves into the landscape of quantum computers, simulators, and relevant programming languages and environments.

Chapter 2 presents the current challenges facing quantum software developers. It examines the inherent complexity of quantum hardware and the need for low-level programming languages, analyzing the complexities that conform to the quantum programming landscape.

Chapter 3 introduces the principles of SOC applied to quantum computing. It explores the emergence of hybrid classical-quantum software service systems and investigates the servitization of quantum algorithms, emphasizing the transformative potential of rendering quantum functionalities as accessible services.

Chapter 4 unveils architectural patterns tailored for quantum computing. Configurations such as Client-Server-Quantum Computer and API Gateway are explored, providing a structural lens for understanding and designing quantum service systems.

Chapter 5 addresses standardization and accessibility, discussing the role of OpenAPI in the generation of quantum services. An OpenAPI extension designed for quantum computing is examined, showcasing practical applications in the standardization of quantum service interfaces.

Chapter 6 details a methodical framework for the development of quantum services. It emphasizes a DevOps approach tailored to quantum services, providing insights into the dynamic and iterative nature of quantum software development.

Chapter 7 proposes an evaluation model designed for the analyzability of quantum software, which includes properties and computational methods for a comprehensive evaluation of the critical aspects that affect the quality and understanding of quantum software.

Chapter 8 presents a summary of key discoveries, and the implications and conclusions drawn from the research are discussed. The chapter also provides a vision for the future directions in the evolving landscape of Quantum Computing as a Service.

Furthermore, a bibliography, showcasing relevant literature and resources, is included for further reading and research

Finally, a comprehensive list of acronyms used throughout the book is provided for quick reference and clarity, as well as a glossary of the most important quantum computing slang.

Intended audience

This book is designed to be accessible to both beginners in quantum and experienced professionals in the field. Its balanced and progressive approach allows beginners and experts alike to find relevant and challenging content throughout its pages.

In this way, the book is intended for a wide and varied audience, from those looking for an introduction to the intersection of classical and quantum software disciplines to experienced professionals seeking to improve their understanding and apply the concepts learned in software engineering.

In essence, this book serves as a valuable learning resource for anyone intrigued by exploring and comprehending the application of quantum computing in the fascinating realm of quantum engineering.

Acknowledgements

This work has been partially funded by the European Union "Next GenerationEU /PRTR", by the Ministry of Science, Innovation and Universities (projects PID2021-124045OB-C31, TED2021-130913B-I00, and PDC2022-133465-I00). It is also supported by QSERV: Quantum Service Engineering: Development Quality, Testing and Security of Quantum Microservices project funded by the Spanish Ministry of Science and Innovation and ERDF; by the Regional Ministry of Economy, Science and Digital Agenda of the Regional Government of Extremadura (GR21133); and by European Union under the Agreement-101083667 of the Project "TECH4E -Tech4effiency EDlH" regarding the Call: DIGITAL-2021-EDlH-01 supported by the European Commission through the Digital Europc Program. It is also supported by the QSALUD project (EXP 00135977 / MIG-20201059) in the lines of action of the Center for the Development of Industrial Technology (CDTI). And by grant PRE2022-102070, funded by MCIN/AEI/10.13039/501100011033 and by FSE+.

We would like also to thank Prof. Mario Piattini for agreeing to write the prologue to this book.

Also, thanks to Ana Díaz Muñoz, Moisés Rodríguez Monje, Manuel Ángel Serrano, Macario Polo, José Antonio Cruz-Lemus and Ignacio García-Rodríguez de Guzmán for writing the Chapter 7 of the book.

Javier Romero-Álvarez

Jaime Alvarado-Valiente

Enrique Moguel

José Garcia-Alonso

Juan M. Murillo

Cáceres, Spain

January 2024

About the Authors

Javier Romero-Álvarez Javier Romero-Álvarez obtained a degree in software engineering in 2020 and the master's degree in computer engineering in 2022 from the University of Extremadura. Currently, he is a PhD student at the same university, focusing his research on quantum computing for the past three years.

He began his research career while still a student in the Software Engineering program, working in the Quercus Software Engineering Group, where he undertook projects related to the development of chatbots and service-oriented computing.

He has participated in different research projects related to quantum computing, such as the projects "QServ: Quantum Service Engineering development, quality, testing & security of quantum microservices" and "QHealth: Quantum Pharmacogenetics Applied to Ageing". These projects aim to integrate quantum aspects into the classical world, seeking ways to bridge both realms and provide real-world applications.

Jaime Alvarado-Valiente Jaime Alvarado-Valiente is a PhD student and scientific research fellow at the University of Extremadura, Spain. He obtained his degree in computer engineering from the University of Extremadura in 2020 and in the master's degree of computer engineering in 2022.

He has been associated with the Quercus Software Engineering Group research group since 2018, where he has developed all his research work. His work and projects within the group have been related to web engineering, service-oriented computing, and chatbot development. In addition, he has served as a substitute professor for nine months in the Department of Computer and Telematic Systems Engineering at the Polytechnic School of Cáceres.

For about three years, he has been researching quantum computing as part of his doctoral thesis, participating in several national projects within the field of quantum computing, such as the projects "QHealth: Quantum Pharmacogenetics Applied to Ageing" and "QServ: Quantum Service Engineering development, quality, testing & security of quantum microservices". These projects show his involvement in pushing the limits of quantum computing and exploring its possible applications in various fields, both health and industrial.

Recently he has been awarded a pre-doctoral contract for doctoral training (FPI) associated with the mentioned QServ project, a proposal developed jointly with the University of Castilla-La Mancha and the University of Deusto for the development of service technology that supports the construction of hybrid classical/quantum systems granted by the Spanish Ministry of Science and Innovation.

Enrique Moguel Enrique Moguel is a computer engineer from the University Carlos III of Madrid (UC3M) and received the master's degree in computer engineering from the University of Extremadura where he won awards for best academic record and best final master's project by the Society of Software Engineering and Software Development Technologies (SISTEDES). He has a PhD in computer science *cum laude* from the University of Extremadura where he won the extraordinary doctoral prize of the university, the award for the best doctoral thesis in Spain in the field of SISTEDES and the award for Innovation in the Drone Sector by the Enaire Foundation.

He has experience in the private sector having worked in companies such as Everis, Telefonica I+D, Airbus, Tecnocom, or Guardia Civil.

Currently, he is an Associate Professor with the University of Extremadura, Spain, where he combines his teaching and research work. He belongs to the Quercus Software Engineering Group.

His main contributions to research and technology transfer have been in the areas of smart systems, the Internet of Things, eHealth, and quantum software engineering. This research work has resulted in more than 60 papers in specialized journals and international and national conferences; 1 patent; 2 utility models; being co-author of several books and book chapters; being founding partner of 2 technology-based companies; etc.

José Garcia-Alonso José Garcia-Alonso receivedhis degree in computer science (2007) from the University of Extremadura. Then, he started his research career in the Quercus Software Engineering Group. In 2014, he received his PhD degree with international mention, and currently he occupies the position of "Profesor Titular de Universidad" at the University of Extremadura.

In the last 10 years, his research interests have revolved around service engineering, mobile computing, the Internet of Things, and quantum software engineering. These interests have materialized in numerous publications in indexed journals and international conferences.

In terms of knowledge transfer to industry and society, he is a founding partner of three technology-based companies and has a utility model.

From these topics, he started a new research line in his group around the use of services to improve the quality of life of aging people. This multidisciplinary topic has also materialized in numerous publications, including several works in different research areas like nursing or gerontology. But more importantly, this research line has been funded with more than 2 million euros from different projects. Particularly, he has been the IP of an Interreg Project funded with more than 1.2 million euros in which he has coordinated five different entities, including three Portuguese universities.

These projects, alongside an interest in quantum computing, allowed José Garcia-Alonso to lead the new research line of quantum service engineering inside his group. Although this line started less than four years ago, it has already materialized in several publications in international conferences and in indexed journals. Similarly, this work, alongside the previously mentioned work with aging people, has attracted the interest of multiple companies in a project funded by CDTI with more than 3.5 million euros focused on the use of quantum services for personalized pharmacogenomics for aging people.

Juan M. Murillo Juan M. Murillo is currently a full professor in the field of software engineering with the University of Extremadura. He develops his research activity within the Quercus Software Engineering Group, which he contributed to creating in 1995. Currently, he leads the SPILab (Social and Pervasive Innovation Lab), which is focused on the development of service technology for mobile devices. Regarding the involvement in services to society, Professor Murillo and his lab are members of the Spanish Network of Excellence Science and Engineering Services. He is also a member of the management board of SISTEDES.

With respect to knowledge transfer to industry and society, Juan M. Murillo was a co-founder and CEO of GLOIN S.L. The company won the Launchpad Denmark, a competition where more than 200 companies from all over the world participated. This allowed the company to run an acceleration process guided by Accelerace in Copenhagen. Prof. Murillo was awarded by the University of Extremadura for his excellence in the knowledge and research results transfer.

Since 2012, the SPILab team has been specializing in building distributed, service-oriented architectures for mobile devices. Their main contributions have been the Internet of People (IoP) concept and the People as a Service (PeaaS) architecture. Both promote considering mobile devices as an infrastructure integrated in the cloud in which services can be deployed. In all this research, the application areas were that of health and aging. Finally, from 2018, the practical problems faced in the field of health have led him to open a new research direction related to the development of software for quantum systems and its integration with classical service-oriented ones.

In this field of quantum software engineering, Juan M. Murillo is currently involved in the development of the QHealth project, which deals with the modeling of systems in the field of pharmacogenomics for the development of precision medicine. This project funded by the Spanish Centre for the Development of Industrial Technology (CDTI) is being developed jointly with the companies Alhambra Consulting, Gloin S.L., and Madrija S.L. Also, as part of the work in this field, he is leading the QServ project. In addition, he has given keynotes on quantum software engineering at several forums such as the International Conference on Service Oriented Computing (ICSOC 2022) or the 2nd Quantum Software Engineering and Technology Workshop (Q-SET 2021).

List of Abbreviations

ADT	Abstract data type
API	Application programming interface
AQ	Auxiliary cubits
AWS	Amazon Web Services
BQP	Bounded-error quantum polynomial time
CC	Cyclomatic complexity
CCG	Circuit gate complexity
CD	Circuit depth
CD	Continuous deployment
CDTI	Centre for the Development of Industrial Technology
CI	Conditional instructions
CR	Coding rule
CS	Class structuring
CuT	Circuit under test
CW	Circuit width
DC	Duplicate code
DevOps	Development and operations
DNS	Domain name system
EDA	Event-driven architecture
HTTP	Hypertext transfer protocol
IaaS	Infrastructure as a service
IoP	Internet of People
IRO	Initialization and reset operations
MO	Measurement operations
MS	Method size
MVC	Model-view-controller
NISQ	Noisy intermediate-scale quantum
PeaaS	People as a Service
PS	Package structuring

QaaS	Quantum Application as a Service
QAOA	Quantum approximate optimization algorithm
QCaaS	Quantum computing as a service
QCC	Quantum cyclomatic complexity
QEC	Quantum error correction
QFaaS	Quantum function-as-a-service
QFT	Quantum Fourier transform
QPU	Quantum processing unit
QSE	Quantum software engineering
QSOC	Quantum service-oriented computing
QTC	Quantum test case
QTC	Quantum test circuit
REST	Representational state transfer
RNN	Recurrent neural networks
RSA	Rivest–Shamir–Adleman
SISTEDES	Society of Software Engineering and Software Development Technologies
SOA	Service-oriented architecture
SOC	Service-oriented computing
SPILab	Social and Pervasive Innovation Lab
TOSCA	Topology and orchestration specification for cloud applications
UML	Unified modeling language
VQE	Variational quantum eigensolver

1

Introduction to Quantum Computing

"What? Are you having any
trouble with quantum
entanglement?"

Captain Fantastic (2016)
Dir. Matt Ross

Quantum computing is a computational paradigm that utilizes the principles of quantum mechanics to process data and solve problems in a different way from classical computing [1]. Its history dates back to the early 20th century when Max Planck postulated the idea of quantized energy, initiating the quantum revolution [2]. However, it was Richard Feynman who first proposed the concept of quantum computing, suggesting that classical computers had limitations in simulating quantum systems and thus necessitated a computer based on these quantum systems to solve this problem [3].

The significant technological advancements of the 21st century have paved the way for the development of quantum computing to become a reality. The manipulation and control of qubits—basic units of quantum information—are essential in this context. These qubits can be in multiple states simultaneously due to superposition, enabling parallel information processing. Furthermore, quantum entanglement, where the information of one qubit is inherently linked to others, adds an additional dimension of complexity and computing capability [4].

Experiments such as quantum teleportation have demonstrated the instant transfer of quantum information between entangled particles, challenging the limits of classical information and opening new possibilities in data transmission and quantum cryptography.

Moreover, major tech companies like Amazon, IBM, Google, or Microsoft are engaged in a race to demonstrate quantum supremacy [5], solving a problem on a quantum computer in significantly less time than it would take on a classical computer. In 2019, Google announced they had solved a problem in 200 seconds on a quantum computer that would have taken the best supercomputers of the time 10.000 years to solve. Two years later, in 2021, IBM announced they had also achieved this feat with their 127-qubit quantum processor named Eagle. Riggetti developed the Aspen-M-3 chip with 80 qubits at the end of 2022, or IBM presented Osprey in November 2022, with a 433-qubit quantum processor. In this regard, IBM, one of the leading companies in the development of quantum computers, has launched Condor with a quantum chip of 1121 qubits at the end of 2023 and plans to launch Flamingo with at least 1386 qubits in 2024, and Kookaburra with no less than 4158 qubits in 2025.

The potential applications of this technology are diverse, ranging from developing more secure cryptographic algorithms to precisely simulating molecular systems for designing new drugs. This technology has the potential to revolutionize areas such as business process optimization, artificial intelligence, economics, health, the discovery of new materials, and even solving complex problems in science and engineering in general [6].

Despite the progress, the design and construction of fully functional quantum computers still face significant challenges [7]. Issues such as qubit stability, error correction, and system scalability are key research areas in this rapidly evolving field.

Continued investment and research by academic institutions, private sectors, and governments are accelerating the development and understanding of quantum computing. Significant milestones are expected in the near future, which will radically transform the processing and manipulation capacity of information on an unprecedented scale.

1.1 Basic Foundations

When delving into the realm of quantum computing, it is imperative to examine a number of fundamental concepts. Within this domain, distinctive properties and processes emerge that offer unique opportunities to leverage computational capabilities. These attributes arise from the deep principles of quantum physics, which distinguish quantum computing as an entirely distinct paradigm.

Thus, quantum computing encompasses a set of principles that revolve around the fundamental postulates of quantum mechanics, such as the use of quantum bits or qubits, and some quantum phenomena such as superposition and entanglement.

1.1.1 Qubit

Just as in classical computing, the basic unit of information is the bit, whose values can be 1 or 0, in quantum computing we have the qubit—or quantum bit. The qubit is the basic unit of information of quantum computing and has the characteristic, and difference with respect to the classical bit, of taking advantage of the quantum properties of matter to have a value of 0, 1, or both at the same time. This latter state is known as a superposition of states—the next concept we will look at—and is what allows us to perform complex computations faster than classical bits. In Figure 1.1, we can see the state comparison between a bit and a qubit.

Mathematically, we can represent a qubit using Dirac's notation [8]. This notation uses a vector of two complex components to represent the state of a qubit and is written as

$$|\psi\rangle = \alpha|0\rangle + \beta|1\rangle. \tag{1.1}$$

Figure 1.1: Difference between qubit and bit.

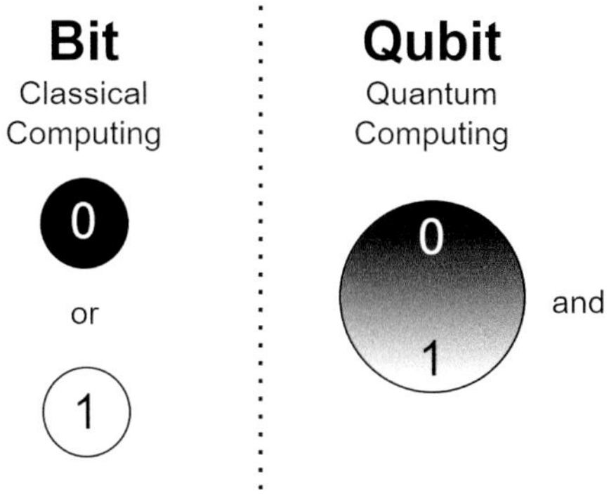

Bit
Classical
Computing

0

or

1

Qubit
Quantum
Computing

0

1

and

In this equation, $|\psi\rangle$ is the state of the qubit, and α and β are complex numbers representing the probability amplitude of finding the qubit in the $|0\rangle$ and $|1\rangle$ basis states, respectively. These states are the computational basis of the qubit and are analogous to the classical 0 and 1.

In addition, it must be satisfied that the magnitude squared of the probability amplitudes α and β sum to 1, which means that the probability of finding the qubit in one of the two states is 1. This can be represented as follows:

$$|\alpha|^2 + |\beta|^2 = 1. \tag{1.2}$$

In addition to the mathematical representation of the qubit, it is common to use the Bloch sphere for its graphical representation—Figure 1.2. In this spherical representation, each point on the sphere corresponds to a single quantum state of the qubit. The upper pole represents the $|0\rangle$ state, while the lower pole represents the $|1\rangle$ state, and the intermediate points on the surface of the sphere represent the superposition of the two base states of the qubit.

The points on the sphere can be described mathematically using eqn (1.1), where the coordinates are related to the probability amplitudes of the qubit.

Figure 1.2: Bloch sphere.

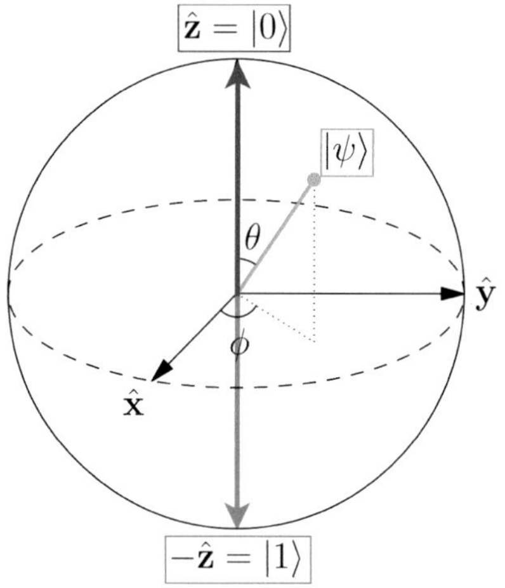

1.1.2 Superposition

Superposition is one of the basic concepts in quantum computing, and it refers to the state in which a qubit can be simultaneously in multiple states, with certain associated probabilities [9].

Superposition allows parallel calculations to be performed in a single step since a qubit in superposition can perform operations in all its possible states at the same time. This means that, if we have two qubits in a superposition state, their combination can simultaneously represent four different classical states (00, 01, 10, and 11) as opposed to the only one we would have with two classical bits—only one of these four. If we extrapolate this to a larger number of qubits, the ability to represent multiple states grows exponentially following the formula $States = 2^n$, where n refers to the number of qubits. This feature is what greatly increases the computational capacity for certain quantum algorithms.

On the other hand, when a measurement is made on a qubit in a superposition state, i.e., its value is observed, its state collapses to one of the classical states (0 or 1) with a probability determined by the probability amplitudes of each state in the superposition. This is a very characteristic aspect of quantum computing: until we do not observe or measure the state of a qubit, it is in a superposition state, and it is at that moment that a definite value is obtained.

The most famous example reflecting the principle of superposition is the one described by Schrödinger, *the Schrödinger cat*. In his article [10], Schrödinger described the following scenario: a cat is placed in a closed box in which a vial filled with poison and a radioactive substance has been placed, which can emit radiation randomly. If this happens, a mechanism is activated that breaks the vial and releases the poison, thus killing the cat.

Figure 1.3: Schrödinger equation for superpositions of quantum states.

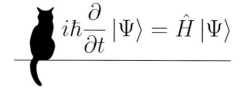

$$i\hbar\frac{\partial}{\partial t}\left|\Psi\right\rangle = \hat{H}\left|\Psi\right\rangle$$

Since the box is closed, it is not known whether the cat is alive or dead. If we open the box and observe the state of the cat, its state will collapse to one of the two probabilities. But until we do so, the cat will be in a quantum superposition, i.e., alive and dead at the same time.

Basically, superposition is one of the characteristics that allow quantum computing to solve certain problems more efficiently than classical systems since it can execute all possible solutions to the problem in parallel.

1.1.3 Entanglement

Quantum entanglement stands as a foundational concept in quantum physics, playing a pivotal role in quantum computing. It describes a unique correlation between entangled particles, such as qubits, that are so intricately connected that the state of one qubit instantly influences the state of the other, regardless of the physical distance between them. This phenomenon defies classical intuition, where the properties of separate entities are independent [11].

In quantum entanglement, if two qubits are entangled, the state of one qubit becomes dependent on the state of the other. Changing the state of one qubit instantaneously affects the state of its entangled counterpart, even if they are light-years apart. This intrinsic connection allows for the creation of entangled pairs, enabling unique quantum computational processes.

Moreover, entanglement introduces a non-locality aspect, meaning that measurements on one entangled qubit provide immediate information about the other, regardless of the spatial separation. This attribute contributes to the speed and efficiency of certain quantum algorithms. However, similar to superposition, the definitive state of an entangled qubit is only revealed upon measurement. Until observed, an entangled qubit maintains its correlated state, demonstrating the intricate and non-intuitive nature of quantum entanglement. This concept is pivotal in quantum computing protocols and lays the foundation for the development of quantum communication technologies.

Quantum cryptography is one of the implications of entanglement [12]. In this case, quantum entanglement serves to ensure secure communication. When two particles are entangled, any attempt at interference or spying would interfere with the quantum state, which would be immediately detected. This provides a method for creating secure quantum encryption keys.

1.1.4 Processes and theorems derived from basic principles

In quantum computing, several processes and theorems are derived from the basic fundamental concepts such as superposition and entanglement, explained above. The most important ones are described below.

Quantum teleportation:

Quantum teleportation is a process derived from the principles of quantum mechanics that enables the instantaneous transfer of the quantum state of one particle to another, without the need for the associated information to travel physically between them. Although it does not involve the material transport of particles, but rather the transfer of information linked to their quantum states, its application in quantum computation and communication is of significant importance.

In this regard, it is a fundamental building block in quantum computing protocols. For example, it is used to transfer information between qubits in quantum circuits. Quantum computers take advantage of teleportation to enable operations and entanglement between distant qubits, even in cases where direct interactions are not possible.

Quantum interference:

Quantum interference is a fundamental phenomenon in quantum mechanics that manifests itself when two or more quantum trajectories combine in such a way that the probability amplitudes of the final results can interfere constructively or destructively. It is essential for many quantum algorithms, such as Grover's quantum search algorithm and Shor's quantum factorization algorithm. These algorithms exploit interference to increase the probability of getting the correct answer and reduce the probability of incorrect answers.

Quantum no-cloning theorem:

The quantum no-cloning theorem states that it is not possible to create an exact copy of an arbitrary quantum state. In other words, one cannot design a universal quantum device that perfectly clones unknown quantum states. This theorem was first formulated by W. K. Wootters and W. H. Zurek in 1982 [13]. This theorem has several important implications in the field of quantum cryptography, one of the most important being the security of quantum key distribution. Moreover, it has fundamental implications in quantum computing because it contradicts the reversibility principle that underlies many quantum algorithms. Understanding these quantum phenomena and taking advantage of these unique properties are the current challenges for software engineers in developing quantum algorithms and technologies. Therefore, in the next section, the concepts for performing quantum programming are shown.

1.2 Quantum Programming using Circuits

The current way we have to design and execute quantum software is through what we call quantum circuits. We can define the concept of a quantum circuit as an abstract representation of the quantum processes we want to occur in a quantum computer.

These circuits are composed of a concatenation of quantum gates, which are unitary operators analogous to the well-known logic gates in classical computing and are described relative to certain bases. Furthermore, they are reversible, which is their most distinctive characteristic.

Visually, the circuits are represented as diagrams showing the sequence of quantum gates—boxes and symbols—applied to the qubits—horizontal lines—to perform specific operations. Generally, quantum circuits are read from left to right, and as we move to the right, the execution of the circuit progresses by applying the gates.

In Figure 1.4, an example of a three-qubit circuit designed with the Quirk[1] tool can be observed.

Figure 1.4: Graphical representation of a quantum circuit.

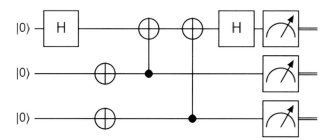

---

[1]https://algassert.com/quirk

1.2.1 Quantum gates of one qubit

Next, we will define the functionality of the main quantum gates for a qubit that we can use in circuits.

Table 1.1: Single qubits gates.

Name	Description
NOT (Pauli-X)	The NOT gate or Pauli-X is the quantum equivalent of the conventional operation of the same name. Zero becomes one, and vice versa. The feature of this gate in quantum processing units (QPUs) is that it can act on qubits in superposition.
	$\lvert 0 \rangle$ —⊕———————— On $\lvert 0 \rangle$ ———————————— Off
Hadamard	It induces superposition in a qubit, crucial for quantum parallelism, and acts as its own inverse, reverting the original state after two applications.
	$\lvert 0 \rangle$ —[H]———————— 50.0% $\lvert 0 \rangle$ ———————————— Off
Phase	It manipulates the relative phase of a qubit through a specific angular rotation, lacking a classical equivalent, and exclusively affecting the state $\lvert 1 \rangle$ of the qubit.
	$\lvert 0 \rangle$ —[(pi/4)]———————— 7.3% $\lvert 0 \rangle$ ———————————— Off

Table 1.1: Continued.

Name	Description
Rotation	The phase gate in quantum computing manipulates the relative phase of a qubit using a specific angular rotation. It is also associated with ROTX—θ—and ROTY—θ—operations, which apply rotations on the X-and Y-axes, respectively.
	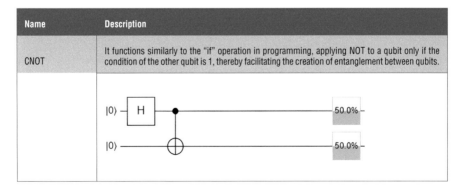
Measurement	Qubit reading process. Its function is to transform the state of a qubit into a collapsed state in a classical bit value.

1.2.2 Quantum gates of multiple qubits

Next, we will define the functionality of the main multi-qubit quantum gates that we can use in circuits.

Table 1.2: Multiple qubit gates.

Name	Description
CNOT	It functions similarly to the "if" operation in programming, applying NOT to a qubit only if the condition of the other qubit is 1, thereby facilitating the creation of entanglement between qubits.

Table 1.2: Continued.

Name	Description
CCNOT	It acts if both control qubits are in state 1. When applied twice, it results in the identity operation. Therefore, it is reversible. CCNOT can be interpreted as an operation that implements "if A and B then rotate C".
CPhase	It generates entanglement through conditional logic. When operated on a register, it rotates—by an angle θ—the $|1\rangle$ values of pairs of operators of a qubit only when another control qubit has the value $|1\rangle$.
CZ	It is typically achieved using the CPhase operation with a specific phase of $\theta = 180$ and is distinguished by its simplified symbol.
SWAP	The functionality of this operation is to exchange the value of two qubits.

1.2.3 Examples of quantum circuits

Understanding the functionalities of the different gates that we can use when defining circuits, this section includes some typical examples of quantum circuits.

1.2.3.1 Adder example

The purpose of the circuit is to add 1 to the number represented in binary format using these qubits. Therefore, the minimum result that can be obtained is 1. In this example, we start with all qubits initialized to 0. Its operation is based on identifying which qubits hold the value 1 and modifying the value of the following qubits. To achieve this, it starts from the least significant qubit, the one with the lowest weight, and checks if it is 0; if so, it changes to 1, and vice versa. Progressing to the next qubit, its value is altered when the previous one is 1. For example, when adding 1 to 1 (decimal), you get 10 (binary). In this case, the first qubit changes from 1 to 0 using a NOT gate, thereby activating the second qubit to 1 using a CNOT gate. The result is 10 (binary) equivalent to 2 (decimal).

By repeating this operation across all qubits, employing a CNOT gate with all the qubits in lower positions, a circuit capable of adding 1 to the number represented by N input qubits is achieved.

An example of this circuit for five qubits can be seen in Figure 1.5.

Figure 1.5: Adder circuit example.

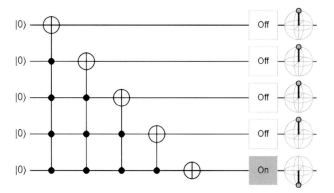

Figure 1.6: Quantum teleportation example.

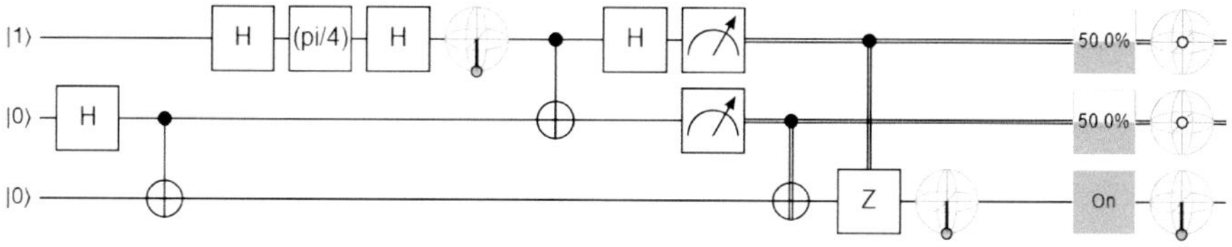

As a curiosity, if in this example with Quirk, all qubits are initialized to 1, the result obtained is 0. This happens because when adding 1 to the binary number 1....1, the result overflows the size of the qubit register we have.

1.2.3.2 Teleportation example

Quantum teleportation is a critical concept for leveraging quantum information. It is the key behind quantum key distribution, long-distance communication, and it is also used in quantum computing. It enables the "teleportation" or movement of a quantum state to another qubit. Quantum teleportation does not involve copying information; it means we "move" the quantum state to another qubit. Quantum teleportation requires three qubits and two classical bits to teleport a quantum state. Since we use three qubits in this example, its complete description requires $2^3 = 8$ basic computational states.

As observed in Figure 1.6, in the first step, qubits 1 and 2—the two bottom lines—are entangled using a CNOT gate. In the second step, the quantum state of the qubit whose value we want to send is prepared using Hadamard and phase gates. Next, the prepared data is linked to the entangled pair by applying a CNOT gate to qubits 0—the top line—and 1. Subsequently, the prepared data from qubit 0 is put into a superposition, and finally, the values of qubits 0 and 1 are measured, that is, the prepared data and the first half of the entangled pair. After measurement, depending on the classical bits of information received by qubit 2, an operation is performed on its qubit.

1.3 Quantum Algorithms

Based on all the concepts that have been mentioned until now, there are a number of quantum algorithms that are well known in quantum computing, and which we will use to develop some examples in the following chapters. These algorithms are the following.

Shor's algorithm:

A well-known problem in classical computing, which forms the basis of security as we currently know it, is the factorization of integers into prime numbers. Algorithms such as RSA or SHA [14]—in their different versions—use the multiplication of large prime numbers to create the public and private keys used, for example, to encrypt connections between a client and a server.

These algorithms are valid today because the complexity of finding the prime factors of a given number is $O((\log N)^3)$, which, translated to the magnitude of the prime numbers used, means that the time taken to "break" a key is greater than the validity period of the encrypted data.

However, in 1994, Peter Shor devised an algorithm that can be executed on a quantum computer—known as Shor's algorithm [15]—which can factor integers in polynomial time with a complexity of $O(\log N)$.

The algorithm consists of several steps:

1. Initial preparation:

    (a) An integer N is chosen to be factored.
    (b) An integer a less than N and which is coprime with N (i.e. the greatest common divisor of a and N is 1) is chosen.

2. Period calculation:

    (a) Quantum computation is used to calculate the period of the modular function $f(x) = a^x \bmod N$.

3. Use of the quantum fourier transform (QFT):

    (a) QFT is applied to the results of the calculations to find the period. QFT is a quantum operator that transforms a periodic function into its frequency representation.
    (b) It allows finding the period of the function $f(x)$.

4. Factors calculation:

    (a) With the information obtained from the previous step, a classic algorithm—such as the Euclidean algorithm—is used to calculate the prime factors of the original number.

Figure 1.7: Shor's algorithm.

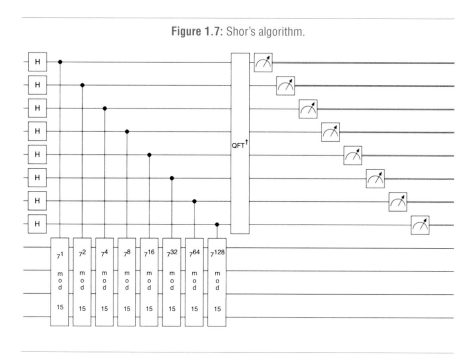

A graphical representation of the circuit for this algorithm for the number 15 can be seen in Figure 1.7, where all qubits are put in superposition, the function $f(x) = a^x \bmod N$ is applied, and finally, the QFT is performed.

Grover's algorithm:

Grover's algorithm [16] is a search algorithm that allows finding—with a probability $> 1/2$—a specific element within a database of N randomly ordered elements using $O(\sqrt{N})$ operations.

The computational cost of solving the problem is determined by the number of calls to the oracle, which is the most significant difference between the classical and quantum cases. The oracle is a function that marks the solution element of the search problem. This function takes as input the indices of the elements and returns a 1 if it is a solution and a 0 if it is not. Therefore, the fewer calls to the oracle needed, the more efficient the search algorithm is.

In this example, the Grover algorithm is presented to solve a search in a list of elements with $x \epsilon N = 2$ qubits. For this purpose, the circuit is organized into the following stages:

Figure 1.8: Grover's algorithm.

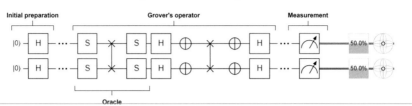

1. Initial quantum state preparation.
2. Oracle.
3. Amplitude amplification.
4. Repeat steps 2 and 3, if necessary.
5. Reading.

The steps to implement the circuit with the previous stages for the state $|00\rangle$ are:

1. The process begins by applying a Hadamard gate to each of the n qubits in the main workspace, which were initially prepared in the state $|0\rangle$.
2. Next, the Grover operator is applied as many times as needed. This subroutine is composed of several gates:

    (a) First, the oracle is applied, formed by CZ and S gates.
    (b) Next, a Hadamard gate should be applied to each of the n qubits in the search space.
    (c) Following that, the CNOT and CZ operators are applied, and then once again, a Hadamard gate is applied to each of the n qubits.

3. Finally, to aid geometric visualization, measurement gates are included.

Deutsch–Jozsa algorithm:

The Deutsch–Jozsa algorithm [17] is a quantum procedure that solves the problem of determining whether a given Boolean function is constant or balanced. Formally, a function $f : \{0,1\}^n \rightarrow \{0,1\}$ is posed, and the objective is to determine if it is constant—returns the same value for all inputs—or balanced–returns 0 half the time and 1 the other half. This algorithm resolves this problem with just a single query to the function, offering an exponential advantage over classical approaches that would require a considerably larger number of queries to reach a definitive conclusion.

Simon's algorithm:

Simon's algorithm [18] operates on two qubit registers, applying transformations controlled by a mysterious and linear function known as f. The algorithm aims to find a vector s such that $f(x) = f(x \oplus s)$, where x is an input value and $\oplus$ denotes the XOR operation. Using quantum transformation operations and final measurements, the algorithm reveals information about the structure of s through a set of results that demonstrate the periodicity in the responses of f, allowing the inference of relevant properties about the function and finding the sought-after vector.

Other quantum algorithms:

Besides the algorithms described previously, there are other algorithms of great importance to the quantum community. Below is a list of the most important and commonly used ones: the Bernstein-Vazirani algorithm, quantum approximate optimization algorithm (QAOA), quantum Fourier transform, variational quantum eigensolver algorithm, HHL algorithm, or the quantum phase estimation algorithm, among others.

1.4 Quantum Computers and Simulators

There are mainly two types of quantum computers with different approaches in terms of operation, applications, and technical challenges: *annealing* and *gate-based* computers.

- **Gate-based:** They are highly versatile and can address a wider range of quantum algorithms. They are suitable for a variety of applications, from factoring large numbers and cryptography to quantum simulations and quantum machine learning, demonstrating broader potential in different areas of quantum computing. They are programmed using quantum circuits composed of specific quantum gates. Currently, this type of computer is where companies are investing the most resources and effort in development.
- **Annealing:** They are highly efficient in solving optimization problems and searching for global minima in functions. These features make them ideal for applications such as route planning or task scheduling, where finding the most optimal solution is crucial.

Among gate-based systems, we can also find *simulators*. These simulators, as the name suggests, simulate the functionality of a quantum computer to test algorithms before implementing them in real quantum hardware. They use a mathematical representation of quantum systems and apply classical computational methods to simulate their evolution, although they are limited by the processing capacity of classical systems.

1.5 Quantum Programming Languages and Environments

Within the quantum computing landscape, this section serves as an introduction to quantum programming languages and environments, describing the most widely used programming languages and software development frameworks specifically tailored to quantum computing. In this way, it is intended to elucidate the tools and approaches that developers can use to be able to program in quantum computing.

1.5.1 Quantum programming languages

Just as in classical computing, in quantum computing, the choice of the appropriate language plays a fundamental role in the effectiveness and performance of developed applications. In this context, two fundamental paradigms stand out: imperative programming languages and functional languages.

Imperative programming languages are characterized by step-by-step instructions that must be executed sequentially to achieve the desired result. In the realm of classical computers, examples of imperative languages include C, JavaScript, Pascal, or Python, among others. Languages for quantum computing encompass many properties similar to these classical languages.

In Table 1.3, a summary of the most important imperative languages for quantum computing is included.

On the other hand, *functional languages* are distinguished by dispensing with step-by-step instructions, relying on mathematical functions to transform inputs into outputs. Despite their lower popularity compared to imperative languages, functional languages present notable benefits. The absence of flow controls and conditionals, such as loop statements or if/else, contributes to simpler error detection and correction. Programmers who focus on writing and reviewing functional code note the ease of identifying errors, as there are fewer instances where unexpected behaviors can be hidden.

These functional languages are characterized by specific features, such as the inclusion of nested functions and the application of lazy evaluation, which defers the evaluation of an expression until its value is needed,

Table 1.3: Imperative languages.

Name	Description
OpenQASM	It is used to perform experiments with low-level quantum circuits. Its syntax has elements of C and assembly languages.
Q#	It implements programs in terms of statements and expressions, much like classical programming languages.
Q|S>	It is a so-called "while-language" language, with the definition of some low-level primitives.
Silq	It is the first quantum language that marks variables as constants and establishes a definition of loops, but the circuit/code part is classical.
QCL	Adopts syntax from languages such as C and Java. It was one of the first quantum programming languages implemented.

thus avoiding unnecessary and redundant evaluations. Among the most used quantum functional languages are Quipper and Pyquil.

Additionally, there is a notable subcategory within functional languages, known as *circuit description languages*, specifically designed for defining quantum circuits. These languages are employed in quantum circuit simulation programs. Notable examples include QuECT, enabling programmers to integrate a circuit into a classical "host" language, and QWIRE, used for defining quantum circuits and providing an interface to manipulate them within a classical "host" language.

Table 1.4 includes the most important functional and circuit definition languages.

1.5.2 Quantum software development kits

Quantum software development kits represent enabling frameworks designed for the development of quantum algorithms, tailored for use in quantum computers or simulation and emulation environments.[2]

Industry leaders, such as Microsoft, IBM, Google, and Rigetti, have actively contributed to the development of open-source development kits. These full-featured toolkits enable software developers to formulate and tackle complex problems in the quantum domain, providing access to simulators and quantum computers through cloud-based platforms.

---

[2]https://research.aimultiple.com/quantum-sdk

Table 1.4: Functional and circuit definition languages.

Name	Description
Quipper	It is a procedural circuit and gate description language, based on Haskell (standardized multi-purpose programming language).
Quil	It is a standard quantum instruction language. Instructions written in Quil can be executed on any implementation of an abstract quantum machine, such as a quantum virtual machine, or on an actual QPU.
LIQUi|>	Developed by Microsoft Research, it allows users to describe quantum algorithms using quantum operations embedded directly in the source code, simplifying the quantum programming process.
QuECT	It is a hybrid approach that allows a quantum circuit to be embedded in a classical "host" program (Java).
QWIRE	A programming language for defining quantum circuits in a modular way, which provides an interface for manipulating these circuits within any chosen classical host language.

Table 1.5: Quantum software development kits.

Name	Description
IBM Qiskit	Is an open-source software development kit that enables users to program, simulate, and run quantum algorithms on real or simulated quantum systems in the IBM ecosystem, all through Python.
Amazon Braket	Allows users to explore, develop, and run quantum algorithms on quantum computers, as well as simulate them on classical computers. Integrated with Python, it provides a platform for quantum computing experimentation and development within the AWS ecosystem.
Cirq	Developed by Google, it provides a Python framework for research in quantum computing, focusing on ease of use, flexibility, and robustness in experimentation and implementation of quantum algorithms.
Quantum Development Kit	Developed by Azure is based on Q#. It enables seamless integration with classical languages like Python and C#, offering tools for quantum computing exploration, development, and simulation within the Microsoft Azure ecosystem.

The deployment of the kits by major companies highlights the commitment to fostering a collaborative and accessible quantum ecosystem. These kits—as can be seen in Table 1.5—not only provide essential utilities for quantum algorithm development but also bridge the gap between classical programming languages, such as Python, and specialized quantum programming languages, such as Q#, a Microsoft offering. So, these kits play a pivotal role in advancing the field of quantum computing by democratically extending quantum capabilities to a broader community of developers, fostering innovation, and accelerating the evolution of quantum software applications.

2

Challenges in Software Development and Deployment of Quantum Services

> "If you think you understand quantum mechanics, you don't understand quantum mechanics."
>
> Nobel laureate Richard Feynman

Due to the emerging state of the quantum software engineering (QSE) field, there is a lack of literature dedicated to the domain of quantum servitization. Nevertheless, there are already some researchers who are beginning to work in this field.

Works like [19] have initiated investigations into the prospective applications of quantum services within the cloud and the research prospects surrounding quantum. Several of the research opportunities presented therein bear resemblance to the issues identified in this study. In particular, the disparities in the implementations of identical quantum algorithms across diverse vendors, and the challenges associated with deploying quantum services on quantum computers.

In the further exploration of quantum service deployment, authors in [20] have advocated for the utilization of a topology and orchestration specification for cloud applications (TOSCA) for the orchestration of quantum services.

TOSCA is a standardized framework for automating the deployment and orchestration of cloud-based applications. In this particular work, the authors have introduced an extension to TOSCA that facilitates the deployment of quantum software. This proposal aligns with the need for a new deployment of quantum applications for each invocation, which requires a conventional computing infrastructure to host and deploy them. Furthermore, it aims to transform the quantum algorithm into a service suitable for integration within a service-oriented architecture.

From a commercial perspective, in conjunction with Amazon Braket platform[3]—a fully managed Amazon Web Services (AWS) service that helps researchers, scientists, and developers get started with quantum computing— there exist alternative propositions aimed at streamlining and standardizing access to quantum hardware and services. Such is exemplified by Azure Quantum,[4] the counterpart to Amazon Braket. Azure Quantum encompasses not only Microsoft and IonQ but also other providers including Honeywell, Quantum Circuits Inc., 1Qloud, and Toshiba. Azure Quantum offers a quantum development kit that facilitates the unification of a heterogeneous array of hardware and software solutions [21].

Similarly, various companies and software developers are actively working on the creation of high-level development environments, toolkits, and application programming interfaces (APIs) aimed at increasing the abstraction level of quantum software. For instance, IBM offers IBM Quantum [22], although it exclusively permits developers to execute quantum algorithms on IBM quantum hardware or simulators. Others in this domain concentrate on specialized areas such as quantum machine learning [23]. However, to the best of the authors' knowledge, these endeavors do not make any notable advances in the realm of quantum services relative to Amazon Braket.

Furthermore, it is imperative to recognize that ensuring the provision of high-quality quantum services necessitates more than just simplifying the development and deployment of quantum algorithms. Additional facets of service engineering, as expounded in works such as [24], must not be disregarded. Specifically, there is a need for substantial efforts in areas such as orchestration, testing, and other facets of quantum service quality [25].

To begin, the foremost consideration pertains to the economic aspect of quantum computing hardware. D-Wave offers its D-Wave 2000Q system, which is currently available for a market price of $15 million,[5] with an impending launch

---

[3]https://aws.amazon.com/braket
[4]https://azure.microsoft.com/products/quantum
[5]https://www.dwavesys.com/resources/white-paper/the-d-wave-advantage-system-an-overview

of its novel advantage model. In contrast, Google's Sycamore chip[6] and IBM's System Q[7] remain absent from commercial availability. However, manufacturers have facilitated access to these systems via cloud-based platforms, supported by APIs. Notably, these quantum hardware configurations exhibit significant bulkiness and necessitate stringent environmental conditions, reminiscent of early historical single-instance computing machinery, such as the ENIAC in 1947 [26], which garnered substantial public interest due to its exorbitant cost of $400,000 and a setup requiring 200,000 man-hours. Although the computational capabilities of these early computers were considerably limited when compared to contemporary standards, they proved adept at solving highly specific problems within controlled conditions, surpassing human capabilities.

The work of programmers of that era was intricately entwined with the peculiarities of the machines they were programming for. Armed with an intimate knowledge of a given machine's idiosyncrasies, programmers developed an array of adroit techniques to optimize its functionality. The resulting programs were challenging to adapt for use on alternative machines and proved inscrutable to other programmers, a phenomenon subsequently christened as "Spaghetti Code" [27]. The contemporary programming landscape surrounding quantum computers bears a striking resemblance to this historical narrative. Given the current limitations of qubits in quantum hardware, programmers primarily engage in experimentation tailored to specific quantum devices, elucidating how these systems can effectively tackle modest, highly specific problem domains. This approach also serves as an invaluable learning experience for programmers seeking to grasp the intricacies of quantum computing.

Analogous to the unreliability associated with early mainframes, which stemmed from their reliance on vacuum tube technology, quantum computers grapple with their susceptibility to instability. Qubits are intrinsically vulnerable to decoherence [28] and various sources of noise, leading to computational errors. Mitigation of these errors necessitates the application of quantum error correction (QEC) techniques, reminiscent of the human intervention required to double-check computations in the past [29, 30]. Consequently, the reliability of quantum computing results hinges on statistical considerations. This predicament underscores one of the central challenges in contemporary quantum computing, namely, the pursuit of stable qubits while diminishing the reliance on error correction measures, a feat that remains uncertain [31].

---

[6]https://quantumai.google/hardware
[7]https://research.ibm.com/interactive/system-one

Surprisingly, the tolerability of programmer tasks was directly contingent upon the confined computational capabilities of the hardware. However, once the computational power of the machinery began to exhibit substantial growth, the situation rapidly degenerated into a state of impracticality. Just like Edsger Dijkstra said when talking about the software crisis "the major cause is... that the machines have become several orders of magnitude more powerful! To put it quite bluntly: as long as there were no machines, programming was no problem at all; when we had a few weak computers, programming became a mild problem, and now we have gigantic computers, programming has become an equally gigantic problem" [32]. Presently, it is recognized that while this observation may have triggered the onset of the software crisis, its fundamental cause resided in the absence of suitable engineering tools and methodologies requisite for software development.

These observations might suggest that the impending prospect of a quantum software crisis is imminent. It behooves the discipline of software engineering to heed these signals and take a proactive stance in its anticipation. Fortunately, we presently possess a reservoir of wisdom cultivated over the past six decades, primarily owing to the endeavors of a distinguished scientific community. An examination of the historical junctures and the judicious decisions that these scientists undertook therein can serve as a valuable compass for guiding prudent progress in QSE. The subsequent section delineates certain junctures that QSE may confront, along with prescriptions drawn from the realm of classical computing to inform optimal decisions.

2.1 Quantum Software Processes and Methodologies

Nowadays, there is no doubt about the interest in QSE [33]. A salient lesson drawn from the trajectory of conventional software engineering is the imperative need for well-defined processes, accompanied by methodological frameworks, which facilitate the execution of various activities within these processes. These activities encompass requirements specification, architectural design, detailed design, implementation, and testing. About the quantum software development process, it is plausible to posit that fundamental strategies employed in classical software development may retain their validity. These strategies furnish a comprehensive blueprint for addressing the challenge of creating software solutions that align with problem requirements. In any scenario, quantum software processes, akin to their classical counterparts, should strive to exhibit qualities of interactiveness, incrementality, and agility.

Nevertheless, it is imperative to scrutinize the methodologies applied to individual activities within the quantum software development process, in light of the distinctive requisites of quantum software. This is necessitated by the fact that techniques devised for classical computing are predicated on an underlying computational model wherein a sequence of instructions operates on a predefined dataset, culminating in a final output state. For instance, the transformation from a requirement specification to a design in the classical paradigm is intrinsically aligned with this computational model. However, this model diverges markedly from the quantum computational model. In quantum computing, there is an absence of a linear sequence of instructions, and instead, we confront a system that exists in a superposition of potential states concurrently. Computational progress halts when a specific subset of the system's state attains a desired configuration, leading to a state collapse that defines the overall system state. Several scholars have already initiated endeavors to formulate methodologies for addressing specific activities, such as design [34], and even re-engineering [35], within the quantum computing domain.

2.2 Abstractions for Quantum Software

An essential prerequisite for the development of novel quantum computing techniques and methodologies lies in the formulation of innovative abstractions within the quantum computational domain. The present discussion will shift its attention toward the conceptual framework of abstraction strategies employed in the creation of conventional software systems.

To illustrate, the incorporation of a class model into a unified modeling language (UML) class diagram entails the representation of a tangible entity from the real-world context. This entity manifests within the system, endowed with the capacity to engage in interactions with other entities. How these interactions transpire is meticulously depicted within a sequence diagram. The utilization of classes is predicated on their proven superior richness compared to the abstract data types (ADTs) that were previously employed. ADTs essentially permitted the modeling of data structures in conjunction with a prescribed set of operations for their manipulation. The rationale for their adoption rested on the recognition that delegating the implementation of data structure operations to individual programmers not only engendered redundant efforts but also introduced semantic disparities within the structures, rendering them arduous to repurpose. Furthermore, both the structures and their associated operations exhibited limited portability across distinct programs. Notably, the functional code became enmeshed with the code responsible for executing operations on the data structures. Consequently, the field of software engineering research realized that a data structure's significance hinged upon the presence of an accompanying set of operations to directly manipulate it.

Preceding the era of ADTs, procedures, and functions were the primary instruments for modeling discrete functional components, allowing programmers to concentrate on their creation, maintenance, and evolution in isolation. In any case, all these abstractions correspond to fragments of software functionality, embodied as sequences of instructions that ultimately manipulate data and interact through a control transfer protocol. This architectural choice stems from the classical computers' foundation in Von Neumann's machine model, which mandates the sequential execution of instructions. Consequently, our models must faithfully encapsulate this reality within the context of the said computer model.

It is pertinent to recall the transition experienced by programmers rooted in procedural programming when transitioning to the utilization of object-oriented classes. Frequently, instances were encountered where classes were crafted to represent data structures analogous to the ADTs they were used to. These classes often grouped diverse modules and were typically complemented by a main class responsible for governing the program's control flow. This tendency persisted even as object-oriented programming literature systematically elucidated the disparities between procedural and object-oriented paradigms. Consequently, it proved to be an arduous endeavor for programmers to modify their conceptualization of software systems, even when the fundamental computer model remained consistent. Therefore, it stands to reason that the impending transition, wherein the underlying computer model deviates significantly, is anticipated to be even more challenging.

Contemplating the transference of our abstractions into the realm of quantum computing engenders a multitude of inquiries. For instance, is the concept of a class applicable within the domain of quantum computing? Does it constitute a suitable abstraction? What motivates the utilization of a class instance in all conceivable quantum states? What is the rationale behind modeling a class in which a segment of its state becomes entangled with that of another class? How can we devise the most suitable abstractions for this endeavor? Undoubtedly, there will be a proclivity to replicate our classical computing techniques and abstractions into the quantum domain. However, akin to the experience of programmers transitioning from procedural to object-oriented paradigms, there is a risk of their improper utilization when attempting tasks fundamentally distinct in nature. Although we shall enable programmers to generate classical computing solutions compatible with quantum computers, we may not necessarily facilitate the cultivation of a quantum mindset and modeling approach [36].

Given the foregoing considerations, it becomes evident that one of the most intriguing avenues for QSE research lies in formulating apt abstractions for the modeling, design, and construction of quantum programs. While contemplating these abstractions, it is also prudent to acknowledge that the class of problems amenable to quantum computing falls under the purview of the BQP class. If these problem typologies can be systematically categorized, it becomes plausible to develop domain-specific modeling languages tailored to address them.

2.3 Quantum Structured Programming

Presently, quantum programming languages [37, 38] predominantly operate at the quantum circuit level, bearing a description reminiscent of the wiring configurations required by the ENIAC for program execution.

One of the most significant advances in the evolution of modern programming languages was the inception of structured programming, which gave rise to fundamental computational constructs: sequence, branching, and iteration. This innovation ushered in a plethora of programming paradigms prevalent in classical computing today.

Analogous to the realm of abstractions, contemplation arises regarding the requisite foundational structures and design motives in the realm of quantum program development. To undertake this endeavor, one must acknowledge the profound divergence between the nature of quantum computing and Von Neumann's architecture model. Researchers have already expressed apprehension regarding this aspect [39, 40].

2.4 Microservices

To comprehensively address the integration of quantum and classical microservices within a unified architecture, a foundational understanding of the operational principles governing extant classical microservices becomes imperative. It is essential to clarify that the present section does not aspire to furnish an exhaustive review of microservices, given the abundance of literature dedicated to this subject [41]. Rather, its principal aim is to furnish a concise portrayal of the operational dynamics inherent to microservices and to deliberate upon the architectural and design patterns necessitating adaptation to facilitate the incorporation of quantum microservices.

Microservices represent a software engineering paradigm that places a primary emphasis on the utilization of services as the foundational building blocks for crafting software solutions [42]. While the literature may present varying definitions and proposals, certain key facets of microservices find widespread consensus.

To begin with, a microservice can be defined as an autonomous entity dedicated to a single responsibility, encompassing both data and logic. These entities are accessible remotely and possess the ability to be independently deployed, modified, substituted, and scaled [42].

The development of microservices solutions allows for the incorporation of diverse computational and storage paradigms [43]. Distinct programming languages, encompassing a mixture of functional and imperative languages, as well as databases, spanning relational and NoSQL databases, are employed to address intricate problems. Microservices do not adhere to a standardized communication mechanism. However, in practical implementation, RESTful HTTP and asynchronous message queues have emerged as the most prevalent means of exposing microservices.

Similarly, while there exists no strict mandate governing the deployment of microservices in terms of location or method, practical implementations predominantly lean toward cloud environments [44]. The cloud's inherent attributes of elasticity and distribution harmonize effectively with the principles underlying the microservices approach.

Finally, despite being entirely separate paradigms not inherently exclusive to microservices, continuous delivery, and development and operations (DevOps), methodologies are routinely applied during the development of microservices systems [45]. Taking all of these considerations into account, it is conceivable that microservices may constitute a suitable choice for a hybrid classical-quantum solution [46]. In this context, recent advances in quantum software development are contributing to the convergence of both realms, particularly from the perspective of cloud computing.

Nowadays, the majority of commercially available quantum computing resources are accessible via cloud-based services, akin to the infrastructure as a service (IaaS) model observed in classical computing. Some studies have coined the term quantum computing as a service (QCaaS) [47] to denote this cloud-based access. Within the purview of QCaaS, developers are allowed to leverage extant quantum computing resources for the execution of their code.

Nonetheless, it is imperative to underscore that this accessibility is markedly contingent on the intricacies of the underlying hardware, necessitating developers to possess a profound comprehension of its idiosyncrasies.

To mitigate some of the limitations inherent to QCaaS and enhance its abstraction level, facilitating the development of intricate quantum software, numerous research and commercial initiatives are currently in progress. In the academic sphere, the nascent discipline of QSE is gaining prominence and captivating the interest of researchers [4, 48]. This field aspires to transplant the knowledge and expertise from classical software engineering into the domain of quantum software development. In particular, certain endeavors are beginning to address aspects of quantum development that bear closer relevance to microservices.

From an alternative perspective, there is an emergence of quantum computing systems exhibiting practical applicability alongside the development of hybrid classical-quantum algorithms (Section 1.3), exemplified by quantum approximate optimization algorithm (QAOA) [49] and variational quantum eigensolver (VQE) algorithm [50].

Furthermore, corporations are actively engaged in the pursuit of more intricate quantum solutions. AWS, a prominent entity in the global domains of cloud and computing services, has established the Amazon Braket platform, which furnishes a developmental environment tailored to quantum software engineers. Amazon Braket extends support to hardware offerings from three distinct vendors, namely D-Wave, IonQ, and Rigetti. D-Wave's machines are categorized as adiabatic quantum computers, while IonQ and Rigetti's offerings fall into the circuit-based quantum computing category. The availability of these diverse computational models augments the array of tools accessible to quantum software developers, albeit it augments the intricacy associated with programming quantum services [51]. For the utilization of adiabatic-based machines, developers are compelled to reformulate their problem statements into the framework of quantum annealing metaheuristic specifications [52]. In the case of circuit-based machines, developers must possess a comprehensive understanding of quantum gates and adapt their problems to suit the quantum circuit framework [53]. This complexity introduces challenges for developers in creating independent, maintainable, and platform-agnostic quantum microservices.

Numerous other companies are also venturing into the development of similar platforms, as evidenced by IBM Quantum, among others. However, to the best of the authors' knowledge, there is currently no proposed solution that adequately addresses the challenges and limitations encountered in the development of quantum microservices to construct hybrid solutions.

3

Quantum Computing as a Service

"The more success the
quantum theory has, the
sillier it looks."

Nobel laureate Albert
Einstein

The microservices architectural style stands as an evolutionary iteration of the service-oriented architecture (SOA) paradigm [54]. The main characteristics are the focus on technical integration issues within SOA applications, which are often described in the form of APIs. In contrast, the microservices approach concentrates on the precise delineation of distinct business capabilities through the implementation of fine-grained business APIs.

Beyond considerations of service design, a pivotal distinction arises in the deployment paradigm. Traditionally, applications have been packaged monolithically, with a development team constructing a comprehensive application addressing all facets of a business requirement. Subsequently, this monolithic application is deployed multiple times onto an application server. In contrast, the microservices architectural style adopts a strategy wherein several smaller applications are independently constructed and packaged, each singularly responsible for fulfilling a specific component of the overall functionality [55].

This chapter aims to explore the emerging paradigm of "quantum computing as a service" by delving into the intersection of quantum computing and microservice architectures. The examination covers a possible implementation of a classical service following existing best practices, design patterns, and standards. Thus, the current state-of-the-art technology for quantum servitization will be analyzed.

3.1 Principles of Service-oriented Computing for Quantum Computing

In a broader context, SOA and the microservices architectural paradigm are not mutually exclusive but can coexist, each bringing distinct advantages.

Specifically, the features offered by microservices architectures are as follows [55]:

- **Loose coupling:** Services are not integrated into the main system, facilitating simplified development and deployment processes. This characteristic allows for independent scalability, and failures can be attached to specific microservices, rather than affecting an entire section or operation of the application.
- **Technological flexibility:** The adoption of microservices does not necessitate radical changes in the technology stack. Each service can leverage the most suitable technology independently of the technologies employed in other microservices.
- **Ease of maintenance and testing:** Microservices, being smaller units focused on specific functionalities, are generally more straightforward to maintain and test.
- **Developer productivity:** Developers find it more accessible to engage and become productive within a microservices environment. Working with several small services, as opposed to a singular complex entity, facilitates seamless integration with DevOps and Agile methodologies.

In contrast, the employment of a microservices architecture introduces certain associated disadvantages, including:

- **Increased complexity:** Microservices systems tend to exhibit higher complexity compared to their monolithic counterparts. Apart from the inherent functionalities of individual systems, the coordination between diverse microservices necessitates addressing varied communication protocols and synchronization mechanisms, thereby augmenting overall system complexity.
- **Challenges in deployment and operations:** Deploying and operating a microservices system is notably more intricate than managing a monolithic system. The coordination and maintenance of different microservices require more effort and coordination from the operations team.
- **Higher computational requirements:** Microservices systems typically require greater computing capabilities than monolithic structures. Despite the optimization potential for

each microservice, the deployment entails distinct containers, dependencies, and replicable components for each service, resulting in aggregated computational demands surpassing those of an equivalent monolithic alternative.

In the realm of software engineering, the development of microservices follows established processes similar to other software artifacts. The microservices architecture has achieved general success in both the software development industry and academia, leading to the emergence of various techniques, methodologies, and tools to aid developers in crafting these systems.

Additionally, specifications such as OpenAPI [56] play a vital role in standardizing endpoints, offering code generation tools that streamline developers' tasks. Once a microservices application is developed, the subsequent steps involve deployment and maintenance, encompassed by the term DevOps [57]. These tasks include integration, testing, administration, and monitoring of microservices.

For traditional systems, deploying a microservices system initiates crucial decisions that significantly impact the architecture's advantages, such as scalability. Considerations include where each service is deployed (multiple services on the same host machine or each service on a different machine), the deployment type (serverless, containers, etc.), orchestration, activity logging, and more [58, 59].

To reduce the complexity of deployment for microservice consumers, the API gateway integration pattern proves invaluable [60]. Serving as the singular entry point for any microservice call, an API gateway functions as a proxy service, directing requests to the relevant microservice. It can aggregate results for consumers, create fine-grained APIs for specific client types, and manage additional aspects like authentication and authorization. This capability empowers developers of microservices systems to handle diverse calls from various channels, support different protocols, and provide responses in varied formats to different clients.

Post-deployment, considerations shift to managing and maintaining services. This involves addressing issues related to communication between services, transaction management, maintaining data consistency, monitoring running services, ensuring security, conducting testing, and attending to numerous other aspects.

While extensive studies and good practices have been established for traditional microservices, a notable gap emerges concerning their adaptation for quantum microservices, highlighting the need to identify practices that seamlessly integrate into the creation of quantum microservices or require specific alternatives [61].

This gap in research becomes particularly significant when considering the principles of service-oriented computing (SOC), a paradigm that leverages services as fundamental elements for software development [62]. SOC, with its focus on SOA, enables the implementation of complex software solutions through a set of services. [63]. Because of this, over the last two decades, SOC, especially web services, has been the focus of intense research, leading to a transition from monolithic software to service-based software running in the cloud [64]. Bridging the established practices of microservices with the emerging field of quantum microservices presents a compelling way for future exploration in this dynamic landscape.

The success of SOC owes much to the evolution of cloud computing, a paradigm designed to offer reliable and customizable dynamic computing environments [65]. Cloud computing's triumph is attributed to its ability to empower companies with cost control, eliminating the need to invest in expensive hardware. Instead, companies can pay for the computing resources they use. The flexibility and scalability provided by cloud vendors allow businesses to instantly adjust their hardware capabilities based on their requirements, making the cloud one of the most successful business models in recent decades [66].

Given the success of the cloud model, it is not surprising that current quantum computers, which remain costly to build and operate, are being offered through a similar paradigm. This model, referred to by some researchers as quantum computing as a service (QCaaS) [47], is akin to the classical infrastructure as a service (IaaS) model in cloud computing. QCaaS allows developers access to existing quantum computers, although this access is highly dependent on specific hardware, requiring significant proficiency in quantum computing to harness its benefits.

To enhance the abstraction level of QCaaS, numerous ongoing research efforts are underway. Commercial platforms like Amazon Braket and QPath[8] provide environments for quantum software engineers, integrating classical and quantum worlds in a quantum development and application life cycle platform for high-quality quantum software.

From an academic standpoint, a new field of research is emerging in QSE, with a focus on translating lessons from classical software engineering to enhance the quality of quantum software [4, 67]. However, as far as

---

[8]https://www.quantumpath.es

current knowledge extends, few works specifically address the perspective of service engineering for quantum and hybrid software. Nevertheless, there are promising initiatives in this domain, such as the proposal of quantum application as a service (QaaS) by Barzen et al. [68], aiming to bridge the gap between classical service engineering and quantum software. These efforts underscore the necessity of adopting a service-oriented approach for the development of quantum services.

In the next section, we delve into a detailed exploration of the life cycle of classical services, with an emphasis on implementation, deployment, and subsequent monitoring and maintenance. Based on best practices, design patterns, and established standards, we aim to provide a view that bridges the gap between the established principles of classical services and the emerging field of quantum services. This exploration lays the foundation for a comprehensive understanding of current tools for implementing quantum services.

3.2 A Good Classic Service Implementation

In this section, we outline a viable approach to supervise the entire life cycle of a classic service. Our comprehensive methodology starts with the implementation phase, progresses through deployment, and extends to the subsequent stages of monitoring and maintenance. To achieve this, we adhere to established best practices, leverage recognized design patterns, and conform to industry standards.

By adopting this approach, we aim to provide a comprehensive guide that not only elucidates the life cycle of a classical service but also establishes a solid foundation for the subsequent exploration of quantum services within a similar framework [69].

The conceptual framework for an exemplary classical service, encompassing implementation, deployment, and monitoring, is depicted in Figure 3.1. It is essential to acknowledge that the definition of a classic service is inherently flexible, allowing for various development approaches. While there is no singular "best" way to delineate a classical service, our endeavor has been to align with widely accepted best practices, prevalent design patterns, and industry standards that have gained prominence in recent years. The approach draws inspiration from the models articulated in [41], an early insight into the realm of microservice architecture.

Figure 3.1: A good classic service implementation.

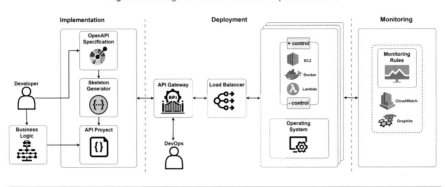

Additionally, we integrate microservice design patterns elucidated by C. Richardson [70], a highly regarded expert in the field of microservices. Complementing these perspectives is the guidance provided by E. Wolff [71], a distinguished software architect with a prolific body of work, particularly in the domain of microservices, as evidenced by his authored books on the subject.

Figure 3.1 is vertically stratified into three layers, each delineating distinct phases in the classical service life cycle. The layer on the left depicts the implementation phase, wherein the service is developed. The middle layer encapsulates the deployment phase, during which the service is published for invocation. The layer on the right illustrates the monitoring phase, where the service undergoes active usage. For each of these phases, we will expound upon the pertinent standards and best practices that characterize classical services.

Implementation phase:

In the implementation of a classic service, developers are faced with two fundamental aspects: the business logic of the service, which is unique for each service, and the API of the service is elaborated.

The OpenAPI specification[9] emerges as a crucial tool for defining the service API. This specification furnishes a standardized, language-agnostic interface to RESTful APIs, empowering both humans and computers to discern and comprehend the service's capabilities without access to source code or extensive documentation. Code generation tools, such as Swagger, can utilize an OpenAPI definition to generate servers and clients in various programming languages. Leveraging OpenAPI, quantum services can be precisely defined

---

[9]https://swagger.io/specification

with their input and output parameters. This definition serves as the basis for generating code stubs, for instance, in Python, wherein the business logic of the service is subsequently incorporated. This approach enables the service to be accessed through a REST request, utilizing JSON to provide input parameters.

Deployment phase:

Once the service is implemented, deployment is imperative for client accessibility. Cloud computing solutions typically serve this purpose, involving the deployment of the API project on hardware provided by a third party. The deployment alternatives range from infrastructure as a service (IaaS) solutions, like Amazon Elastic Compute Cloud (EC2), offering complete control over a virtual machine, to container-based approaches such as Docker, and serverless paradigms like Amazon Lambda, where no control over the underlying infrastructure is granted to service creators. Regardless of the deployment method, the service will exhibit some level of coupling with the operating system of the deployment environment.

Simultaneously, a prevalent design pattern in classical service deployment is the API gateway [72]. Essentially, the API gateway consolidates all API requests from clients, discerns the requisite services, and amalgamates them into a unified, seamless experience for users. In this context, the quantum service would be invoked through the back-end API gateway, which transmits the request to the corresponding service and delivers the computed response.

Monitoring phase:

Upon deployment and invocation by users, continuous monitoring by the DevOps team becomes essential to ascertain the service's capability to handle the demand. To address this, a load balancer can be employed in conjunction with the API gateway. Concurrently, monitoring rules can be defined, and tools such as Graphite[10] or Amazon CloudWatch[11] can be utilized to obtain fine-grained insights into the service's status. This monitoring framework facilitates control over the service's status, request volume, infrastructure costs, and other critical metrics, ensuring the service's robust performance and efficient resource utilization.

The details of the development, deployment, and monitoring processes depicted in Figure 3.1 might appear extensive, potentially raising the question

---

[10]https://graphiteapp.org
[11]https://aws.amazon.com/cloudwatch

of whether all these components are necessary for a simpler service. However, each component serves a specific purpose, and the adoption of these patterns and best practices in SOC is rooted in their collective contribution to the overarching benefits of service orientation. Foremost among these benefits are:

1. **Platform independence:**
   Adopting a REST API, grounded in HTTP, IP, and other internet protocols, facilitates platform independence. Services can be invoked from any platform, irrespective of the service language, client language, or the platforms on which they operate. The utilization of JSON for data transfer ensures compatibility across various implementation languages. The OpenAPI specification further enhances this independence, defining a well-formed, consumable API accessible by any client.

2. **Location independence:**
   Classical services exhibit independence not only in their deployment locations but also at two distinct levels:

   - **Physical independence:** REST, HTTP, and DNS afford physical independence, enabling service invocation through a URL regardless of the deployment location.
   - **Logical independence:** An API gateway conceals the complexity within a more intricate project, providing logical independence for a given service and streamlining accessibility for service clients.

3. **Decoupling:**
   Decoupling is achieved on three fronts:

   - **Decoupling between services:** The API gateway facilitates communication between different services within a single API, allowing services to interact without direct knowledge of each other.
   - **Decoupling between services and hardware:** The platform on which services are deployed (e.g. EC2, Docker, Lambda) ensures decoupling between services and the underlying hardware and operating systems.
   - **Decoupling between services and programming language:** The OpenAPI specification and code generation tools enable decoupling between services and the programming languages in which they are written. Service stubs can be generated in different programming languages, fostering language-agnostic interoperability.

4. **Scalability:**
   Ensuring scalability is crucial for addressing dynamic changes in demand. Elastic platforms, coupled with a load balancer capable of initiating and terminating service instances as needed, provide an economically efficient solution to achieve scalability.

5. **Composability:**
   Services must be composable, allowing a collection of simple services to coalesce and solve complex problems. The API gateway, proficient in decomposing a single invocation into calls to different services without the services' awareness, facilitates this composability.

6. **Reliability:**
   Reliability, encompassing security, maintainability, accountability, and other facets of service robustness, is paramount. A comprehensive set of monitoring and analytic tools becomes indispensable, furnishing the requisite information about the services to ensure their reliability across various dimensions.

To take advantage of these benefits, it is necessary to create a complex infrastructure, such as the one illustrated in Figure 3.1. However, based on the current understanding of the authors, there appears to be a notable absence of dedicated support for harnessing the advantages of SOC when one of the services within an API is implemented as a quantum service.

With all this in mind, considering the complexities of quantum computing, including its distinctive computational principles and models, this presents an environment that demands specialized considerations in the context of service-oriented environments.

As quantum computing continues to evolve, it becomes imperative to explore and develop frameworks that seamlessly integrate quantum services into the broader SOC framework, ensuring the realization of its benefits across the quantum-classical divide. From this arises the question, what is the current situation for quantum servitization?

3.3 What Is the Current Situation for Quantum Servitization?

In the conventional realm of SOC, the process of substituting one service for another, even across different hardware architectures, is generally straightforward. This transition is facilitated seamlessly when the entire infrastructure, as depicted in Figure 3.1, is well-established. However, the dynamics change significantly when there arises a necessity to replace a classical service with a quantum counterpart.

To explore this uncharted territory, a parallel methodology is adopted, akin to the one employed in defining classical services. The objective is to transpose the classical architecture into the quantum domain, preserving the quality attributes inherent in SOC. This endeavor involves a meticulous analysis of each facet within a hybrid classical-quantum architecture.

In the realm of the ***implementation layer*** for a quantum service, the imperative task is the realization of the service business logic, reflecting the established practice for classical services. Within this layer, in alignment with conventional implementation practices, a primary requirement is platform independence. This is achieved through the adoption of a REST API, relying on HTTP, IP, and other well-established internet protocols, ensuring seamless communication between services. Likewise, the utilization of JSON serves as a standardized means for data transfer between services, independent of the underlying implementation languages. The OpenAPI specification plays a crucial role in fostering this independence, offering a framework for defining a well-formed API that is easily consumable, as mentioned in the previous section. However, the quantum implementation realm currently lacks defined communication protocols, standardized formats for interlinking classical and quantum services, and established specifications for crafting APIs to ensure service independence. Chapter 5 addresses this gap by presenting our proposition for defining quantum services, introducing an extension to the OpenAPI specification.

Furthermore, researchers have started to address these intricate challenges. For instance, Cuomo et al. [21] provides a comprehensive overview, shedding light on the primary challenges and open problems encountered in designing a distributed quantum computing ecosystem, particularly from the vantage point of communications engineering. Their work delves into the complexities associated with communication within the quantum realm, contributing valuable insights to the evolving discourse. In a parallel vein, Rojo et al. [51] tackle the challenge of translating theory into practice by presenting an implementation in the form of a quantum microservice for a prominent problem—the prime factorization problem with Shor's algorithm. Their efforts exemplify a practical exploration of quantum services, offering a glimpse into the potential applications of quantum computing within the realm of service-oriented architectures.

Another pivotal facet of SOC is decoupling, particularly at the implementation layer where the separation must exist between services and the programming language in which they are written. For classical service development, this decoupling is effectively facilitated by the OpenAPI specification and code generation tools like Swagger. These tools adeptly generate the service stub in various programming languages, ensuring language-agnostic interoperability. Conversely, in the realm of quantum service design, the absence of standardized specifications and code generation tools to generate the stub structure of an API project poses a notable challenge. Chapter 5 of this book also addresses this crucial aspect by leveraging the

OpenAPI code generation tool to generate quantum services compatible with various commercial platforms, providing a foundational step towards achieving decoupling in quantum service implementation.

Another noteworthy contribution in this domain is the work of Dreher and Ramasami [73], who have developed a prototype container-based system. This system empowers developers to prototype, test, and implement quantum algorithms with enhanced agility and flexibility.

In the *deployment layer*, current options include various commercial platforms capable of executing quantum algorithms. Notably, platforms like Amazon Braket offer the execution of quantum algorithms in different simulators or on quantum processors. However, certain limitations exist, such as the lack of granular control over the platform where quantum services are executed. For instance, in Amazon Braket, only one quantum task can be queued for a quantum processor, awaiting a response. The forthcoming Section 3.3.1 provides an illustrative example of servitization, demonstrating the integration of a quantum algorithm within the Amazon Braket platform.

Within this layer, it is crucial that services maintain independence from the deployment location. From a classical service design standpoint. At the physical level, location independence is facilitated by REST, HTTP, and DNS, allowing services to be accessed via a URL regardless of their deployment location. Simultaneously, at the logical level, the API gateway plays a pivotal role in ensuring location independence within more intricate projects, shielding clients from the underlying complexity. Chapter 4 of this book presents a quantum API gateway, aligning with the traditional API gateway pattern while tailoring it to the quantum realm. This quantum API gateway not only conceals complexity but also dynamically recommends the optimal quantum computer for executing a given quantum service at runtime. This multifaceted challenge has also been addressed by Kumara et al. [74], who introduced a vision of quantum service-oriented computing (QSOC). This model envisions the construction of hybrid business applications by fostering collaboration between developers of classical services and developers of quantum services.

Another pivotal characteristic of SOC in the deployment layer is decoupling. Examining classical service design, two different types of decoupling are considered essential. Firstly, there is the decoupling between different services within the same API, facilitated by the API gateway. This gateway proficiently communicates between services without necessitating direct awareness between them. Secondly, there is the decoupling between services and the underlying hardware and operating systems, orchestrated by the platform on which the services are deployed (e.g. EC2, Docker, Lambda). Chapter 6 of this book introduces a DevOps approach for the continuous deployment (CD) of quantum services, leveraging Docker containers and tools like GitHub Actions to streamline the deployment process.

In tandem with this effort, Grossi et al. [75] contribute to this trajectory by delineating an architectural framework. This framework addresses the challenges associated with integrating an API-exposed quantum provider into an existing enterprise architecture. Furthermore, they present a minimum viable product solution, effectively merging classical and quantum computers within a basic scenario. The reusable code, housed in a GitHub repository, signifies a practical step toward fostering the integration of classical and quantum computing resources within enterprise architectures.

Concluding at the ***monitoring layer***, the current landscape for monitoring quantum services presents a notable gap. In classic service monitoring, a multitude of tools such as Graphite or CloudWatch are available. However, the scenario is less promising when it comes to monitoring quantum services. The absence of dedicated tools for this purpose highlights a significant shortfall in the existing quantum computing ecosystem. The development of specialized monitoring tools for quantum services holds substantial potential, offering considerable benefits in acquiring detailed insights into the state and performance of quantum services.

In essence, the resilience and scalability of services are imperative to effectively address customer demand. The conventional approach involves leveraging elastic platforms and a load balancer capable of dynamically initiating or terminating instances of the service as required, ensuring optimal resource utilization without incurring excessive costs for the cloud provider. However, the development of similar capabilities in the quantum realm is in its nascent stages. Initial efforts in this direction, as highlighted in earlier discussions and forthcoming proposals in subsequent chapters, underscore the ongoing exploration of scalable and resilient quantum services.

3.3.1 Quantum algorithm servitization

Based on the principles of classical SOC, where distribution and servitization of development have already demonstrated significant benefits, the application of quantum computing becomes particularly compelling, as explained before. This transition to quantum computing does not deny the knowledge learned from classical SOC. Instead, it raises an exploration of how quantum algorithms can be distributed and servitized, echoing the successful patterns established in the classical computing paradigm.

To delve into the present landscape of quantum services, this section opts for the utilization of Amazon Braket. Amazon characterizes Braket as a fully managed quantum computing service. In precise terms, Amazon Braket furnishes a comprehensive development environment that facilitates the construction of quantum algorithms. It further enables the testing of these algorithms on quantum circuit simulators and the execution of the algorithms on diverse quantum hardware technologies.

Given that Amazon presently holds a global leadership position in cloud computing and services technologies through AWS, leveraging Amazon Braket emerges as a compelling choice for the development of quantum services. Despite the homogeneity in the current state of quantum software development across different platforms, similar outcomes can be anticipated if quantum services were to be developed on alternative platforms.

So, in the realm of SOC, the fundamental unit is a service, a self-describing, platform-agnostic computational element that facilitates the agile and cost-effective composition of distributed applications [62].

However, Amazon Braket, in its current state, does not directly focus on offering developed quantum algorithms as services that can be invoked through an endpoint for the construction of more intricate applications.

To overcome this limitation, a viable solution is to encapsulate the quantum algorithm within a classical service. This involves incorporating a classical computer to execute the classical service, which, in turn, invokes the quantum computer. As far as the authors are aware, there is presently no direct means of invoking a quantum algorithm as a service. Figure 3.2 illustrates an example of this approach. Specifically, the code of the quantum circuit responsible for creating Bell states [76] between two qubits, a fundamental and well-known quantum computation, is encapsulated within a Flask[12] service. Deployable on a classical computer, this Flask service provides a straightforward mechanism for integrating quantum algorithms into a sophisticated service-oriented solution.

Next, we present a more complex quantum algorithm servitization in order to illustrate the actual situation of quantum services that can be developed on Amazon Braket.

---

[12]https://flask.palletsprojects.com/en/3.0.x

Figure 3.2: Bell state quantum algorithm wrapped by a classical service.

```
from flask import Flask, send_file
from flask_cors import CORS            Amazon Braket
import matplotlib.pyplot as plt        Libraries
# AWS imports: Import Braket SDK modules
from braket.circuits import Circuit
from braket.devices import LocalSimulator

app = Flask(__name__)                  Classical
CORS(app)                              Service

@app.route('/execute', methods=["get"])
def execute_quantum_task():            Quantum
                                       Algorithm
    # build a Bell state with two qubits.
    bell = Circuit().h(0).cnot(control=0, target=1)
    device = LocalSimulator()
    result = device.run(bell, shots=1000).result()
    counts = result.measurement_counts
    # print counts
    print(counts)
    plt.clf()
    plt.bar(counts.keys(), counts.values())
    plt.xlabel('bitstrings')
    plt.ylabel('counts')
    plt.savefig("result.png")
    return send_file("result.png", mimetype='image/png')

if __name__ == '__main__':
    app.run(host="localhost", port=33888)
```

3.3.1.1 Example of servitizing integer factorization using Amazon Braket

Between the several applications, we have decided to tackle integer factorization, more precisely with a particular application of the later denoted prime factorization. The problem selected is a problem well known by the scientific community working in quantum computing and, at the same time, is simple enough to be comprehended by any newcomer.

While integer factorization is computationally demanding, it does not fall within the NP-hard class of problems, as established by Jiang et al. [77]. Nevertheless, its significance is underscored by its foundational role as a hardness assumption in cryptographic algorithms, exemplified by the widely used RSA algorithm. Therefore, advancements in tackling integer factorization carry considerable weight in the realm of information security.

Numerous proposals and algorithms exist for solving this problem, with Shor's algorithm being the most prominent [15]. Shor's algorithm, formulated in terms of quantum gates and circuits, is well-suited for execution on platforms like IBM's Q computing chip [78]. However, alternative approaches to quantum computing, such as adiabatic quantum computing based on quantum annealing, cannot directly implement Shor's algorithm. In this context, alternative algorithms for prime factorization gain prominence, such as the one proposed in [79]. In this study, the chosen algorithms for integer factorization encompass Shor's algorithm for quantum machines utilizing quantum circuits and gates [80, 81]. Additionally, we explore integer factorization based on quantum annealing for adiabatic quantum machines, exemplified by D-Wave's approach [23].

To provide a practical demonstration of quantum services that can be developed on Amazon Braket, we have implemented the aforementioned integer factorization algorithms on this platform.

As of the time of writing this book, Amazon Braket offers support for seven distinct quantum computer simulators and real quantum computers from three diverse hardware vendors. Notably, the supported quantum computers include several providers employing a quantum circuit-based development approach—IonQ, Oxford Quantum Circuits, QuEra, and Rigetti[13].

The integer factorization algorithms have undergone rigorous testing on all the supported quantum machines and simulators within the Amazon Braket ecosystem.

Given that the supported simulators within the Braket ecosystem are also grounded in quantum circuits, Shor's algorithm has been successfully implemented on both simulators and quantum circuit-based hardware. Figure 3.3 presents a segment of the quantum period-finding subroutine of Shor's algorithm implemented using Amazon Braket. It is noteworthy that the entire circuit for Shor's algorithm can be executed seamlessly across all three simulators and the two circuit-based quantum computers supported by Braket. However, it is worth mentioning that certain operations, such as measurement and qubit reinitialization, supported by many other existing simulators and often found in public implementations of Shor's algorithm, are not supported by Amazon Braket. In the figure, this part of the algorithm is commented out as an illustration. Adapting Shor's algorithm to circumvent the need for these operations requires additional effort to tailor one of the most well-known algorithms to the specifics of a given quantum platform.

---

[13] https://docs.aws.amazon.com/braket/latest/developerguide/braket-devices.html

Figure 3.3: Fragment of the quantum circuit needed to run Shor's algorithm in Amazon Braket.

```python
app = Flask(__name__)

def shor(N, a):
# N = Integer to factor (currently 15, 21, 35 work)
# a = Any integer that satisfies 1 < a < N and gcd(a, N) = 1
    shors_circuit = shors_algorithm(N, a)
    local_simulator = LocalSimulator()
    output = run_shors_algorithm(shors_circuit, local_simulator)
    guessed_factors = get_factors_from_results(output, N, a)

    return (guessed_factors)

@app.route('/shor_simulator_sv1', methods=['GET'])
def shor_simulator_sv1():
    N = int(request.args.get('N'))
    a = int(request.args.get('a'))
    shors_circuit = shors_algorithm(N, a)
    managed_sim = AwsDevice("arn:aws:braket:::device/quantum-simulator/amazon/sv1")
    output = run_shors_algorithm(shors_circuit, managed_sim)
    guessed_factors = get_factors_from_results(output, N, a)

    return jsonify(str(guessed_factors))

if __name__ == '__main__':
    app.run(debug=False, port=8080)
```

While the quantum circuit remains consistent across various quantum hardware or simulators, the method of invoking the algorithm varies depending on the execution environment. Figure 3.4 illustrates the Amazon Braket invocation code for the three simulators and the two supported quantum computers. As depicted, invoking the algorithm using the local simulator is the most straightforward. However, when running the algorithm on other simulators, an Amazon Simple Storage Service S3 destination must be defined to store results, along with a timeout for polling these results. In contrast, when executing the algorithm on real quantum computers, a recovery task must be defined. Quantum algorithm execution is an asynchronous operation, and developers are responsible for retrieving results.

In the case of executing integer factorization on an adiabatic quantum machine, a complete algorithm rewrite is necessary. Adiabatic machines, rooted in the adiabatic theorem closely linked to quantum annealing, require a distinct mapping approach compared to gate-based machines, rendering quantum

Figure 3.4: Fragment of the Amazon Braket code to invoke the Shor's algorithm in different devices.

```
if(selected_device=="LocalSimulator"):
    device = LocalSimulator()
    return device.run(circuit, shots=1000).result()
elif (selected_device=="SV1"):
    device = AwsDevice("arn:aws:braket:::device/quantum-simulator/amazon/sv1")
    return device.run(circuit, s3_folder, shots=1000, poll_timeout_seconds=24*60*60).result()
elif (selected_device=="TN1"):
    device = AwsDevice("arn:aws:braket:::device/quantum-simulator/amazon/tn1")
    return device.run(circuit, s3_folder, shots=1000, poll_timeout_seconds=24*60*60).result()
elif (selected_device=="Rigetti"):
    device = AwsDevice("arn:aws:braket:::device/qpu/rigetti/Aspen-8")
    task = device.run(circuit, s3_folder, shots=1000, poll_timeout_seconds=5*24*60*60)
    return recover_task_result(task)
elif selected devices =="ionQdevice"):
    device = AwsDevice("arn:aws:braket:::device/qpu/ionq/ionQdevice")
    task = device.run(circuit, s3_folder, shots=1000, poll_timeout_seconds=5*24*60*60)
    return recover_task_result(task)
```

circuits unsuitable. These examples, though small, underscore the current state of quantum software from the standpoint of SOC.

In conclusion, these examples highlight the intricacies and adaptations required in the current landscape of quantum software development within the SOC paradigm. The diverse architectures and nuances across quantum hardware and simulators necessitate careful consideration and customization in the implementation and invocation of quantum algorithms, underscoring the evolving nature of quantum software within SOC.

4

Architectural Design Patterns for Quantum Computing

> "Quantum software development concept emerges from quantum programming languages."
>
> Prof. Jianjun Zhao

4.1 Architectural Design Patterns

Architectural design patterns are reusable solutions to commonly occurring problems in software architecture [82]. In the context of quantum computing, these patterns can help architects to organize and structure quantum software systems in a way that takes advantage of the unique properties of quantum mechanics [4].

Many existing architectural design patterns have been developed and used in classical software systems. Each pattern has its strengths and weaknesses, and architects must choose the appropriate pattern for their specific system and requirements. Here are some examples [83]:

- **Layered architecture:** This pattern involves organizing the system into a series of layers, each with a specific responsibility. For example, a typical layered architecture might include a presentation layer, a business logic layer, and a data access layer. Each layer communicates with the layer above and below it, and the overall system is designed to be modular and flexible

- **Client-server architecture:** This pattern involves dividing the system into two parts: a client part that interacts with the user, and a server part that performs the processing and storage. The client and server communicate with each other over a network, and the overall system is designed to be scalable and distributed.

- **Model-view-controller (MVC):** This pattern involves dividing the system into three parts: a model that represents the data and business logic, a view that displays the data to the user, and a controller that handles user input and updates the model and view. The MVC pattern is commonly used in web applications and other user interface-heavy systems.

- **Microservices architecture:** This pattern involves breaking the system down into a collection of small, independent services that communicate with each other over a network. Each service is responsible for a specific task, and the overall system is designed to be scalable, flexible, and resilient.

- **Event-driven architecture (EDA):** This pattern involves designing the system to respond to events, such as user input or system events. The system is designed to be loosely coupled, with components communicating with each other through events rather than direct method calls.

- **Pipe and filter:** In this pattern, the data is processed linearly, with each filter performing a specific operation on the data and passing it on to the next filter. The filters are typically designed to be independent of each other, with each filter performing a specific task and not relying on the state of other filters.

- **API gateway:** This pattern is responsible for handling all client requests, including authentication and authorization. The gateway then routes the requests to the appropriate microservices in the system, based on the request type and the data being requested.

One example of an architectural design pattern that has a quantum counterpart is the layered architecture pattern. In classical software systems, the layered architecture pattern involves organizing the system into a series of layers, each with a specific responsibility. In the context of quantum computing, this pattern can be adapted to take advantage of the unique properties of quantum mechanics. For example, a layered architecture for a quantum computing system might include layers for quantum gate operations, quantum error correction, and classical control logic. Each layer would be responsible for a specific aspect of the quantum computing system and would communicate with the layers above and below it [39].

Another example of an architectural design pattern with a quantum counterpart is the pipe and filter pattern. In classical software systems, this pattern involves processing data through a series of filters, each of which performs a specific operation on the data [84]. In the context of quantum computing, the pipe and filter pattern can be used to process quantum data through a series of quantum gates, as presented by Killoran et al. [85]. In this work, a quantum computing system uses a pipe and filter architecture to perform a QFT, which is a fundamental operation in many quantum algorithms. The filters in this case are quantum gates, and the pipes would represent the flow of quantum data between the gates.

In this way, the predominant quantum software architecture patterns currently recognized are the layered pipe and filter patterns. However, it should be noted that these patterns are generic and are commonly used in the design of classical software systems. They do not specifically focus on attributes of quantum computing such as superposition and quantum entanglement. Consequently, there is a pressing need for new research efforts aimed at *identifying and proposing new patterns* tailored to take advantage of quantum features [83]. These new patterns should be aimed at optimizing the architecture of quantum software systems by taking advantage of the distinctive features of quantum computing.

Some exemplary patterns that show the potential for improvement of quantum software architecture include:

- **Quantum circuit architecture:** One approach to this pattern is in which quantum operations are arranged sequentially, similar to the structure of classical electronic circuits. Each quantum operation, often represented as a gate, is applied to specific qubits, and the overall arrangement defines the flow of quantum information. The pattern encompasses the sequential execution of quantum gates, resulting in the creation of a quantum circuit. This pattern has significant application in quantum algorithms where the sequence and order of quantum operations are crucial to achieving the desired computation. Examples include algorithms such as Shor's algorithm (Section 1.3), which involves a series of quantum gates arranged in a specific circuit to efficiently factor large numbers.
- **Client-server-quantum computer architecture:** This pattern would integrate the classical client-server architecture with the unique characteristics of quantum computing, offering a structured approach to QSOC. It would establish a framework for interaction between classical clients and quantum servers, enabling the integration via hybrid systems of quantum algorithms and computations in classical computing environments. So, this pattern introduces a hybrid architecture that combines classical client-server components with quantum computing entities. This fusion would enable the utilization of quantum capabilities within existing classical computing infrastructures.
- **Entanglement-superposition architecture:** This pattern would take advantage of the unique quantum phenomena of entanglement and superposition to optimize the design and execution of quantum algorithms. By intertwining these quantum features, the pattern aims to enhance parallelism, promote efficient information processing, and enable the development of advanced quantum applications.

As discussed above, in the broader context, architectural design patterns constitute a potent instrument for architects involved in the design of quantum computing systems. Through the modification of classical design patterns to leverage the distinctive properties inherent in quantum mechanics and the design of new quantum patterns, architects can devise systems that surpass classical counterparts in terms of efficiency, flexibility, and scalability. The subsequent section, Section 4.2, delineates an adaptation of the API gateway pattern specifically designed for the quantum domain.

4.2 Adaptation of the API Gateway Pattern for Quantum Computing

The API gateway pattern, traditionally employed for microservices composition in applications, functions as an entry point to the system, directing requests to various microservice routes. It can apply filters to incoming requests, aggregate results, and implement specific logic. In a notable adaptation presented in [86], the API gateway is enhanced with machine learning capabilities, enabling it to recommend the most suitable quantum machine based on user-indicated parameters within the request. Essentially, this adaptation optimizes the deployment strategy of a quantum service dynamically.

For this proposal, the quantum API gateway is implemented in Python, utilizing the Flask library for defining the API with distinct endpoints. The project is presently hosted on an AWS server and offers a reference implementation for Amazon Braket. Ongoing efforts are directed toward expanding its coverage to include other quantum computing providers, such as IBM Quantum [87].

Additionally, integration with Google and Microsoft platforms is currently in progress, aiming to realize the envisioned system illustrated in Figure 4.1. This development marks a significant enhancement in the deployment and execution efficiency of quantum services.

At present, the tool leverages information furnished by the quantum computing providers regarding the status of execution queues on their respective machines. Utilizing this data, the quantum API gateway intelligently deploys quantum services on the most suitable machine and platform, adhering to the user's specified constraints. This approach ensures that the quantum API gateway deploys quantum services in a constraint-aware manner, independent of the underlying infrastructure. Upon receiving user requests, the gateway processes them and returns responses in a standardized format applicable across all quantum computing providers.

Figure 4.1: Quantum providers solutions through quantum API gateway.

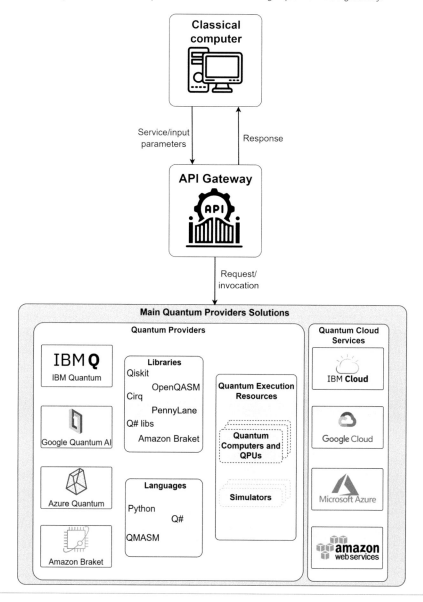

The execution process, as portrayed in Figure 4.2, commences with a classical machine initiating a call to invoke a quantum service (step 1). This service request encapsulates a comprehensive set of input parameters

Figure 4.2: Quantum API gateway process.

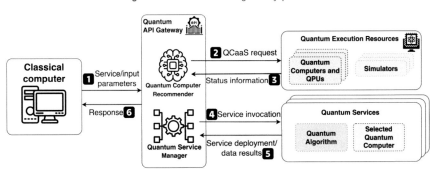

and optimization specifications tailored for the quantum machine. These parameters include considerations such as the desired number of qubits, the maximum acceptable cost for execution, and the preference for a specific machine type—whether annealing or gate-based.

Upon the reception of the service call, the quantum API gateway springs into action, establishing communication with the QCaaS provider to procure real-time information about the current status of available quantum machines (step 2). Leveraging its advanced recommender system, the quantum API gateway systematically evaluates and analyzes the gathered information to select the most optimal machine for the deployment of the requested service (step 3). This crucial decision-making process is influenced by various factors, including the specified constraints and requirements outlined in the service call.

Having identified the optimal machine, the quantum API gateway seamlessly orchestrates the deployment of the quantum service on the chosen quantum machine (step 4). Subsequently, the quantum API gateway diligently assembles the response generated by the quantum service, presenting it in a standardized format for coherent communication with the classical machine (step 5). This standardized format ensures a uniform and consistent response interface irrespective of the underlying quantum hardware.

As the execution concludes, the quantum API gateway plays an additional pivotal role by providing valuable feedback to its quantum machine recommender. This feedback loop is integral for the continuous refinement and optimization of future machine selections, enriching the recommender's understanding and adaptability based on the accumulated insights from each service execution (step 6). Through this iterative process, the quantum

Figure 4.3: Algorithm for the section of the best quantum computer.

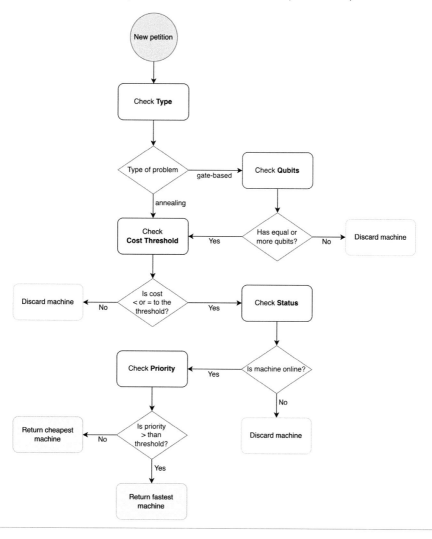

API gateway endeavors to enhance the overall efficiency and effectiveness of quantum service deployment within the broader quantum computing ecosystem.

Therefore, the quantum API gateway, following the algorithm outlined in Figure 4.3, brings notable advantages over existing approaches to utilizing quantum services. It provides developers with the flexibility to dynamically choose between different quantum service providers at runtime, considering factors like the required number of qubits for the computation. This decision-making process relies on information from the quantum service providers, be it static data, as in Amazon Braket, or dynamic backend information, as in IBM Quantum. Additionally, the tool allows the selection between gate-based and annealing-based machines, enhancing efficiency in quantum computing without compromising precision.

Moreover, the quantum API gateway, beyond considering the number of qubits, assesses the cost implications associated with the chosen quantum computer. This evaluation incorporates various factors such as the developer's specified number of shots, the maximum cost threshold set by the developer, and the cost per shot. Here, "shot" represents the number of iterations required to discover the solution and retrieve the results of the service execution. This comprehensive cost analysis ensures that the chosen quantum service provider aligns with both the computational needs and budget constraints defined by the developer.

In determining the service execution cost, the tool integrates the cost per run with the cost per shot, multiplied by the specified number of shots. The tool exclusively opts for machines falling within the cost threshold, with this information readily accessible from certain providers like Amazon Braket. Nevertheless, some providers currently do not furnish this information dynamically. In such instances, a cost estimate is derived from the technical specifications. Subsequently, the selection of the supplier is determined based on availability, ensuring a judicious choice in the absence of real-time cost data.

Once the developer identifies machines meeting the cost threshold, the quantum API gateway conducts a thorough check of the quantum computers available that fulfill these criteria. Subsequently, it computes the estimated execution time for each machine, providing the developer with crucial insights for a well-informed decision. This estimation is based on the context of execution established during the provider comparison, encompassing factors such as the day of the week, the initiation time of the execution, and the historical duration of previous executions performed on that specific computer.

In essence, this meticulous process guarantees the selection of the most cost-effective and efficient machine for running the quantum service. Consequently, with these enhancements to the tool, we ensure the optimal machine is chosen for every service call. By enforcing a standardized format for service responses and integrating a feedback mechanism for the quantum machine recommender across diverse providers, the entire execution process is streamlined. This approach empowers developers to abstract from the intricacies of both quantum machines and providers.

It is worth noting that this implementation of the quantum API gateway is designed with modularity in mind. The static and dynamic characteristics, along with those considered when estimating execution time, can be supplemented with various parameters from other providers. Similarly, the method for analyzing time estimation information can be replaced or parameterized with different values, enhancing the adaptability and flexibility of the system.

4.2.1 Execution time forecasting model

The execution time forecasting model, implemented with Keras, serves to predict the total execution time, encompassing both the waiting time and the actual execution time. This model utilizes available information and context parameters to calculate the execution time, employing two distinct models: one tailored for gate-based machines and another for annealing machines. The division into two models is essential as each incorporates specific parameters corresponding to its machine type.

Furthermore, the execution time is not solely contingent on the characteristics of a specific execution but is also influenced by the task load on the quantum processor. To address this, a temporal analysis is conducted on the recent executions performed on each machine. This analysis considers the characteristics and time requirements of each execution to forecast the execution time. Notably, the temporal analysis focuses on the historical performance of the processor, as Amazon Braket, at the time of this paper, does not provide real-time workload evolution.

The implementation leverages deep learning techniques, specifically neural networks, with a preference for Recurrent Neural Networks (RNN) [88]. RNNs are chosen for their ability to retain data memory and, more specifically, long short-term memory is employed due to its superior long-term memory compared to traditional RNNs. Although specific metrics of model quality are omitted here due to space constraints, it is crucial to note that alternative network architectures can be substituted without affecting the quantum API gateway's functionality. The impact would primarily be on the accuracy of time estimations for quantum service execution.

4.2.2 Functionalities of the quantum API gateway

To realize the functionalities outlined above, the quantum API gateway incorporates two key endpoints, each serving distinct purposes. The first, accessible through a *GET* request to /execute, orchestrates the optimization process within the quantum API gateway. It utilizes the specified input parameters and, upon completion, returns the most suitable quantum computer for executing the given code.

On the other hand, the second endpoint, available through a *POST* request to /feedback, enables users to communicate the execution time for a specific service on a particular quantum computer. This communication includes details such as the executed service's description encompassing qubits and shots, as well as contextual variables like the day of the week and the time of the day. This feedback mechanism serves the purpose of refining the execution time estimation model within the quantum API gateway. These structured endpoints collectively contribute to the adaptive and learning capabilities of the quantum API gateway, enhancing its overall efficiency and effectiveness in quantum service deployment.

Thanks to this, the quantum API gateway stands as a valuable tool for developers, offering users a tailored quantum computing experience that aligns with their specific requirements. Whether the priority is cost efficiency or swift execution, the quantum API gateway provides recommendations to run on a quantum machine that optimally balances the desired features with the associated costs. In instances where speed is crucial, the gateway suggests the machine with the shortest execution times. This ensures that, regardless of the scenario, the most suitable quantum machine is consistently identified and presented as a recommendation. Moreover, by structuring quantum API gateway as a REST API, its seamless integration with other service deployment tools is facilitated, enhancing its adaptability within contemporary software development frameworks and methodologies.

In summary, the quantum API gateway effectively tackles the challenge posed by the unique nature of quantum computing, where services cannot be pre-deployed on a quantum computer for subsequent execution. The gateway introduces an innovative solution to this constraint by offering optimization capabilities. This empowers developers to dynamically identify the most fitting quantum computer for each execution of a quantum service at runtime, overcoming the inherent limitations associated with the deployment of quantum services.

5

Generation of Quantum Services

> "No language which lends
> itself to visualizability can
> describe quantum jumps."
>
> Nobel laureate Max Born

As discussed in previous chapters, in the realm of quantum computing, programming languages often resort to circuit-based models, introducing lower and less intuitive abstractions. This challenge is compounded by the need to account for the distinct characteristics and functionalities of individual quantum machines [89]. To address these complexities and enhance quantum programming, the field of QSE is actively exploring techniques that not only address programming intricacies but also grapple with design and requirements challenges inherent in quantum systems [90].

These challenges prompt the exploration of alternatives that can elevate quantum tools to a level comparable to classical ones, with the ultimate goal of achieving a higher level of abstraction, obtaining quality processes, and facilitating the development of hybrid classical-quantum systems [91]. Encouragingly, existing tools already offer more abstract and simplified approaches to interfacing with diverse quantum machine providers [87].

In the pursuit of advancing quantum programming and bridging the gap between quantum and classical computing, the development of more efficient and accessible processes becomes imperative. Nevertheless, current tools predominantly consist of programming libraries for quantum computers, demanding a profound understanding of the technology due to the absence of standardized practices. To overcome this limitation, we propose the utilization of the OpenAPI specification[14] for the generation of quantum services.

The objective is to create quantum applications that facilitate a higher level of abstraction during the development phase. Leveraging this specification enables the amalgamation of classical and quantum computing, encapsulating quantum processes within classical methods and functions [92]. Consequently, this approach facilitates the invocation of a quantum circuit, treated and executed as a service.

5.1 Standardization and the OpenAPI Specification

Standardization plays a pivotal role in the realm of software development, providing a framework for consistency, interoperability, and ease of collaboration [93]. This significance is especially pronounced in the context of service-oriented architectures, where disparate components need to seamlessly interact with one another. The need for standardization arises from the inherent complexity and diversity of modern software systems. As services become integral components of complex systems, ensuring a uniform and comprehensible approach to their implementation, documentation, and invocation becomes imperative.

One of the primary motivations for standardization is the diverse technology landscape. In the world of web services, heterogeneity exists not only in terms of programming languages but also in the underlying infrastructure, data formats, and communication protocols. Without standardized practices, integrating services across this diverse landscape becomes a daunting challenge [94]. Standardization provides a common language and set of conventions, enabling developers to articulate service interfaces consistently.

Thus, to interact with external services, understanding their APIs becomes essential, and contemporary services often adopt the RESTful web services (web APIs) paradigm [95]. To make these services accessible, defining their APIs is imperative. In this context, the OpenAPI framework has gained increasing popularity among developers, primarily due to its generators, which contribute to maintaining consistency in the implementation and documentation of services [56].

---

[14]https://swagger.io/specification

Figure 5.1: Classical services definition process with OpenAPI specification.

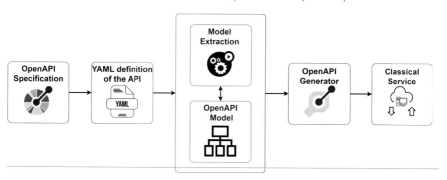

While OpenAPI has emerged as a widely adopted framework for API specification and standardization, it is essential to acknowledge that alternative approaches have been explored within the realm of service standardization. Some noteworthy alternatives include RESTful API Modeling Language, API Blueprint, and GraphQL.

When implementing a classic service through OpenAPI, developers amalgamate two crucial aspects: the business logic, which embodies the service's functionality, and the service's endpoint, delineating how an external client can invoke it.

The OpenAPI specification serves as a language-independent standard interface for RESTful APIs. This specification facilitates both human and machine comprehension of a service's capabilities without requiring access to source code, documentation, or network traffic inspection. It plays a pivotal role in defining the service and outlining its input and output parameters. Developers can leverage this specification to generate the code structure of a web service using a source code generator, allowing flexibility in choosing their preferred programming language. Subsequently, developers can augment the generated code with the requisite business logic, rendering the web service fully functional and operational [56]. Figure 5.1 shows an example of standardization and generation of classic services using the specification.

Moreover, employing OpenAPI enables the definition of the recover private key service along with its input and output parameters, followed by the generation of a code stub, for instance, in Python. This code stub provides the foundational structure to which developers can add the specific business logic for the service. Adhering to this approach allows the service to be accessed through a REST request, with JSON used to convey the input parameters. While OpenAPI stands as a robust solution, it is worth exploring alternative approaches to standardization, ultimately leading to the adoption of OpenAPI for its proven benefits in fostering consistency and comprehensibility in service implementation and documentation.

5.2 Scaffolding of Quantum Services

To tackle the existing challenges in quantum service development, we leverage OpenAPI in a manner analogous to its application in classical service implementations. In particular, we have adapted the OpenAPI Code Generator[15] to accommodate the intricacies of defining and constructing quantum web services. The OpenAPI Code Generator, developed by the OpenAPI initiative, serves as a web-based tool enabling the generation of server applications and client APIs based on an OpenAPI specification. Comprising various modules and a collection of libraries, this tool delineates the code generation process for diverse programming languages.

To realize this integration into quantum computing, we have developed an extension to the OpenAPI specification, incorporating custom properties. Simultaneously, we extended the OpenAPI Code Generator to facilitate the definition and code generation for quantum applications. The graphical representation of the service generation workflow is depicted in Figure 5.2, with the following steps involved.

5.2.1 Define quantum business logic

The *initial step* involves articulating the business logic of the service as a quantum circuit using Open Quirk.[16] This entails specifying either the Open Quirk URL of the generated circuit or directly providing a URL containing the source code in Qiskit[17] language, which can be obtained from the IBM Quantum Composer.[18]

For the integration of quantum service business logic, we employ a graphical quantum programming tool that supports drag-and-drop functionality for constructing quantum circuits. Open Quirk, our chosen quantum circuit composer, is an open-source solution developed in JavaScript. Its purpose is to

---

[15] https://openapi-generator.tech

[16] https://algassert.com/quirk

[17] https://qiskit.org

[18] https://quantum-computing.ibm.com/composer

Figure 5.2: Quantum services definition process with OpenAPI specification.

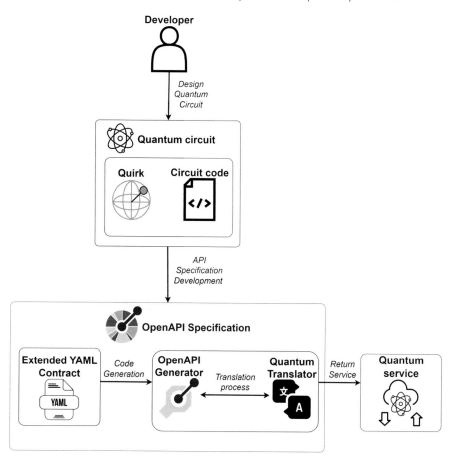

streamline the rapid prototyping of quantum circuits, offering both graphical editing capabilities and programmatic access to the composed quantum circuit. It is worth noting that Open Quirk can be substituted with any other tool facilitating quantum circuit creation, provided it offers programmatic access to the code, allowing seamless integration with the OpenAPI specification.

As an alternative to graphical circuit editors, we offer the flexibility to include quantum circuits directly in the service endpoint through a URL where the code is located, such as Qiskit code. This versatility enhances the adaptability of the quantum service composition process.

5.2.2 Define quantum service endpoints with OpenAPI

The *second step* involves the definition of quantum API endpoints using OpenAPI. This step requires establishing an API contract, where each endpoint corresponds to a distinct API method, and each endpoint integrates its unique business logic. Connecting the previously defined quantum circuit with the specific endpoint intending to access that business logic is crucial. To accomplish this, it is imperative to incorporate, into the YAML specification of the API, either the Open Quirk URL of the circuit or the URL where the Qiskit code is situated. This API definition adheres to the standard YAML file used by the OpenAPI specification, providing comprehensive information about the API, including available endpoints, paths, and potential operations on each path.

The OpenAPI specification has been expanded to accommodate quantum circuits, introducing custom properties (also known as specification extensions or provider extensions). These properties facilitate the inclusion of supplementary information in the API contract definition. Consequently, a quantum service can be automatically generated from a quantum circuit and an OpenAPI specification enriched with custom quantum properties. These properties allow specifying the link where the circuit is located and the desired quantum provider for service generation.

Figure 5.3 illustrates a segment of the YAML API contract, showcasing custom properties and parameters appended to the specification. The inclusion of these custom properties enables the description of additional functionalities beyond the standard OpenAPI specification. The first property, labeled *x-quantumCode*, serves to store the URL with the generated circuit code or the Open Quirk URL. The second property, *x-quantumProvider*, empowers developers to specify the service provider where the service will be executed, with current options being IBM Quantum or Amazon Braket–providing Qiskit as a development kit and services of Amazon Braket, respectively.

This second property is included in the specification instead of being an option in the code generation tool to permit developers, as explored later, to create quantum APIs with services running on different vendors within the same specification. This flexibility is crucial due to the incompatibility of machines from different vendors, varying in qubit count and pricing.

Furthermore, two essential parameters—*machine* and *shots*—have been incorporated into the specification for the accurate execution of quantum services. The *machine* parameter, also depicted in Figure 5.3, allows the service client to dynamically select the specific machine where the quantum algorithm

Figure 5.3: Fragment of the YAML API contract.

```yaml
paths:
  /circuit/ShorAWSquirk:
    get:
      tags:
        - quantum_code
      summary: Get the circuit implementation of Shor Algorithm
      description: ''
      operationId: ShorAWSquirk
      parameters:
        - name: machine
          in: query
          description: Shor's algorithm is a quantum computer algorithm
                       for finding the prime factors of an integer
        - name: shots
          in: query
          description: Number of shots
      responses:
        '200':
          description: successful operation
        '405':
          description: Invalid execution
      x-quantumCode: 'https://algassert.com/quirk#circuit={"cols":[["H","H"
      x-quantumProvider: 'aws'
```

will be executed from those available at the provider specified in the *x-quantumProvider* custom property. This capability is particularly important for providers like Amazon Braket and IBM Quantum, which offer an array of quantum computers to developers.

For example, Amazon Braket provides simulators (*LocalSimulator, TN1*, and *SV1*) and real quantum computers (*IonQ, Borealis, Lucy, Rigetti Aspen-8, Rigetti Aspen-9, Rigetti Aspen-11*, and *Rigetti Aspen-M-1*). With the *machine* parameter, clients can dynamically choose the machine at runtime. Notably, the results of the quantum algorithms' execution will be stored in an Amazon S3 storage (specific to this provider). The generated code encompasses both the endpoints and the configurations for result storage, eliminating the need for developers to manage the storage and retrieval of the results explicitly. These configurations ensure that results are delivered upon request during service invocation.

Moreover, IBM Quantum offers a diverse range of over 20 cloud-connected systems. Customers with a premium plan gain access to the most advanced systems at their convenience, while an open plan provides free access to less advanced quantum systems for the public.

Furthermore, the *shots* parameter provides the flexibility to specify the number of circuit executions to be performed on the chosen quantum machine with each service request. This parameter allows users to control the level of precision and detail in the results obtained from the quantum algorithm.

5.2.3 Generate quantum service source code

In the *third step*, the extended OpenAPI Code Generator comes into play, generating the source code for the quantum services. This code generator leverages a translator API to construct the code based on the provided quantum circuit.

Upon specifying the quantum API, the OpenAPI Code Generator automatically produces the source code for the quantum services. To accomplish this, we extended the tool with a new library (*python-quantum*) built on the existing Python library designed for generating APIs with Flask. Flask is a widely used and lightweight Python web application framework. Consequently, the generated quantum API endpoints are implemented in Python, utilizing Flask. Each of these generated endpoints is responsible for deploying and executing the corresponding quantum algorithm on the machines specified by the developer, as indicated by the custom properties incorporated into the OpenAPI specification.

So, these endpoints encapsulate the source code required to execute a quantum task on the specified provider and machines. The source code of the quantum task is also generated, tailored to the designated provider, and is based on the quantum circuit specified in the *x-quantumCode* property.

5.2.4 Deployment of quantum services

Finally, in the *fourth step*, the generated quantum services are ready for deployment and invocation through RESTful calls to the endpoints encapsulating the quantum algorithm code.

Figure 5.4 illustrates the generated code for the Grover algorithm, designed to run on Amazon Braket, encapsulated within a classic Flask endpoint. The generated source code encompasses the necessary libraries of the quantum provider, a classical wrapping service, and the available machines supported by the quantum provider. Additionally, it includes the business logic derived from the quantum circuit translated into the language supported by the quantum provider.

The translation process is facilitated by an intermediate system deployed as a translator, ensuring accurate and efficient translation while proficiently handling the intricacies of quantum programming languages.[19] This translator

---

[19]https://github.com/JaimeAlvaradoValiente/openapi-generator-quantum

Figure 5.4: Quantum service for Amazon Braket wrapped in a classic endpoint.

```
from braket.circuits import Circuit                      Amazon Braket
from braket.devices import LocalSimulator               Libraries
from braket.aws import AwsDevice

def showAWSQuirk(machine, shots):  # noqa: E501                         Classical
    """Get the circuit implementation of Shor Algorithm                Service
    # noqa: E501
    :param machine: Name of the machine where to execute
    :type machine: str
    :param shots: Number of shots
    :type shots:

    :rtype: None                                              Amazon Quantum
    """                                                      Computers and S3
    gate_machines_arn= { "riggeti_aspen8":"arn:aws:braket:::device/qpu/rigetti/Aspen-8",
                         "riggeti_aspen9":"arn:aws:braket:::device/qpu/rigetti/Aspen-9",
                         "riggeti_aspen11":"arn:aws:braket:::device/qpu/rigetti/Aspen-11",
                         "riggeti_aspen_m1":"arn:aws:braket:us-west-1::device/qpu/rigetti/Aspen-M-1",
                         "DM1":"arn:aws:braket:::device/quantum-simulator/amazon/dm1",
                         "sv1":"arn:aws:braket:::device/quantum-simulator/amazon/sv1",
                         "tn1":"arn:aws:braket:::device/quantum-simulator/amazon/tn1", "local":"local"}
    s3_folder = ("amazon-braket-7c2f2fa45286", "api")
    circuit = Circuit()
    circuit.reset(0)
    circuit.reset(1)
    circuit.reset(2)
    circuit.x(0)
    circuit.x(1)                    Quantum
    circuit.x(2)                    Algorithm
    circuit.cnot(1,2)
    circuit.cnot(2, 1)
    circuit.cnot(1,2)
    circuit.cnot(0,1)
    circuit.cnot(1,0)
    circuit.cnot(0,1)
    return executeAWS(s3_folder, gate_machines_arn[machine], circuit, shots)
```

incorporates an endpoint for each supported provider, receiving the Open Quirk URL, formatting it, and generating the code using the gates specified in the corresponding language. The specific quantum machine, in which the algorithm will run, is provided by the service client as a parameter.

The generated API is deployable on a classical computer and provides a high-level abstraction for service-oriented solutions to incorporate quantum algorithms. Accessing these algorithms is achieved through classical REST requests, where the service is invoked via HTTP methods, as depicted in Figure 5.5.

Execution of these quantum services is contingent on quantum hardware providers such as IBM Quantum or Amazon Braket. When clients issue requests to the API endpoints, these services initiate the execution of the corresponding quantum algorithm on the selected quantum hardware provider.

In summary, this process allows developers to build quantum services exposed through a RESTful API, thus making them accessible to other services

Figure 5.5: Executing a quantum service endpoint derived from generation with OpenAPI.

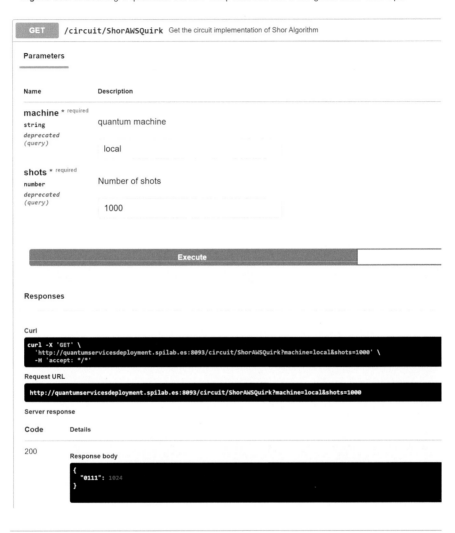

or applications. It combines the principles of service-oriented architecture with quantum computing, making quantum computing a versatile and accessible quantum computing infrastructure.

6

DevOps for Quantum Computing

> "Those who are not shocked
> when they first come across
> quantum mechanics cannot
> possibly have understood
> it."
>
> Nobel laureate Niels Bohr

The integration of quantum services with classical counterparts introduces distinctive challenges, primarily rooted in the inherent constraints of quantum systems. Despite the advancements outlined in preceding chapters, a noticeable void exists in the literature concerning the development of quantum services. This gap underscores the pressing requirement for tools and methodologies that can empower quantum service development, mirroring the capabilities accessible for classical cloud services [96]. The lack of available resources imposes limitations on developers, challenging their ability to create and deploy quantum services efficiently [91].

This chapter addresses this discrepancy by bridging the gap between the development of quantum services and classical cloud services. Our approach is to adapt existing tools and methodologies to the specific needs of quantum services development. A pivotal aspect of our strategy is the introduction of a comprehensive pipeline designed for the generation and deployment of quantum services. Drawing inspiration from the principles of the DevOps methodology, particularly continuous software integration, our proposed pipeline enhances the OpenAPI specification modification introduced in the preceding chapter. Notably, we incorporate the automation of the continuous deployment (CD) process to deploy services in readily consumable containers [97, 98].

The implementation of this workflow for continuous software integration and deployment leverages techniques and tools related to the DevOps methodology. In the following sections, we describe this deployment process, explaining in detail its development and functionality.

DevOps, characterized by its focus on collaboration, automation, and communication between development and operations teams, plays a pivotal role in enhancing the speed, quality, and reliability of the software delivery process [99].

In the context of quantum software development, the application of DevOps becomes even more crucial due to the distinct challenges posed by quantum computing [100].

6.1 Significance of DevOps Methodologies in Quantum Development Processes

Quantum software undergoes more rigorous testing and validation compared to classical software, primarily owing to the impact of errors introduced by noise in quantum states [101]. Here, DevOps emerges as a key facilitator, offering automation solutions for testing and validation processes, contributing significantly to the heightened reliability of quantum software [102].

Quantum software is inherently more complex and computationally intensive than its classical counterparts. To manage this complexity effectively, DevOps practices come to the forefront by automating crucial tasks such as deployment, scaling, and maintenance. By doing so, quantum software development becomes more efficient and scalable, aligning with the principles of DevOps [103].

Among the core practices of DevOps, continuous integration (CI) and continuous deployment stand out [104]. CI involves the seamless integration of code changes into a shared repository, fostering collaborative development. On the other hand, CD automates the deployment of software updates to the production environment as soon as they are deemed ready. The integration of these practices into quantum computing is exemplified by H.T. Nguyen et al.'s work [105] on quantum function-as-a-service (QFaaS) and the introduction of a unified life cycle.

Furthermore, research efforts are actively exploring the intersection of quantum computing and DevOps. Gheorghe-Pop et al. [102] bring about an adaptation of the traditional DevOps process to quantum DevOps, focusing specifically on testing the reliability of noisy intermediate-scale quantum (NISQ) devices. In the commercial realm, Microsoft has incorporated DevOps techniques into its cloud computing platform, Microsoft Azure, for quantum computing.[20]

However, despite the progress made in integrating quantum computing with DevOps principles, a notable gap persists in the availability of practical tools and implementations to support developers in quantum DevOps practices. While various proposals effectively incorporate quantum algorithms into distinct phases of the DevOps cycle, there remains a significant void, especially in addressing pivotal aspects related to the build and deploy phases. These phases, widely acknowledged as integral components of the DevOps life cycle, encompass the intricate processes of creating software packages and orchestrating their seamless deployment in the production environment [91].

Our ongoing research endeavors are strategically positioned to fill this void by concentrating on the optimization of the build and deployment processes. By delving into these critical phases of quantum DevOps, we aspire to enhance the efficiency and agility of quantum computing application delivery. Through the development of practical tools and implementation strategies, our goal is to enable developers to build quantum software packages and deploy them robustly, thus contributing to the advancement of quantum DevOps practices and facilitating the wider adoption of quantum computing technologies.

6.2 Deployment of Quantum Services using DevOps Techniques

In this section, we delve into the deployment of quantum services, aligning with DevOps principles to improve efficiency and reliability throughout the software delivery life cycle.

To commence the deployment of automatically generated quantum services, it is imperative to pre-configure the environment with the essential credentials from service providers. These credentials, usually provided by entities like AWS or IBM, encompass crucial elements such as passwords, secret keys, and specified regions. This preliminary configuration ensures seamless accessibility and unlocks the full functionality of the deployed quantum services.

---

[20] https://learn.microsoft.com/es-es/azure/architecture/guide/quantum/devops-for-quantum-computing

Figure 6.1: Workflow for the deployment of quantum services.

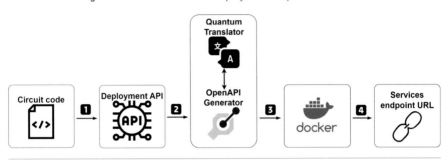

Embracing the principles of DevOps, the deployment process leverages the power of containerization, with Docker playing a pivotal role. Containers provide an isolated and consistent runtime environment, ensuring that quantum services function reliably across diverse deployment scenarios. The use of Docker facilitates deployment automation, a key of DevOps practices.

The proposed deployment workflow, depicted in Figure 6.1, adheres to the CD philosophy of DevOps.

The main element of the automated deployment process is the deployment API, an API designed to streamline the creation and deployment of containers seamlessly. Deployed on an AWS server, this API runs the pipeline detailed in the previous chapter, dedicated to generating quantum services.

The steps are described below in the context of a DevOps-centric approach:

- **Steps 1, 2, and 3: Input configuration and service generation.** Upon receiving a request, the deployment API initiates the process of generating quantum services, drawing inputs such as the desired application name, a YAML file modified from the OpenAPI specification, and essential configuration parameters for the providers. This aligns with the principles of CI in the DevOps methodology, ensuring that each generated service integrates into the existing codebase.
- **Step 4: Containerization and Dockerfile preparation.** The fourth step involves encapsulating our dynamically generated quantum services within Docker containers. This step not only ensures the portability of our services but also streamlines the deployment workflow through automation. So, this Dockerfile serves as a blueprint, outlining the sequence of commands and configurations necessary for creating a self-contained and portable quantum service environment.

  The Dockerfile encapsulates more than just the quantum service code: it encapsulates the entire execution environment and dependencies. This ensures that the quantum service runs smoothly in different computing environments, mitigating issues related to specific system configurations.

As a result, developers can deploy quantum services without worrying about compatibility or environmental-related issues.

To enhance replicability, we provide a base container in the repository.[u] This base container is a complete Python image, configured to encompass all essential dependencies required for running quantum services. By pre-installing these dependencies, we eliminate the inconvenience of manual installations, ensuring consistency and reliability across multiple computing environments.

- **Step 5: Port assignment and deployment.** The deployment process culminates with the assignment of a port on the server. The system checks available ports against a predefined list and assigns the first available one. DevOps principles of automation and efficiency shine through in this step, ensuring that the deployed services are accessible through the assigned port.

---

[u]https://hub.docker.com/r/jromero236/quantumservices

6.3 Automation for Continuous Deployment Making Use of GitHub Actions

In the realm of CD, we have crafted a pipeline to integrate the automatic generation of quantum service code with its deployment in containers, poised for consumption by users. At the heart of this implementation lies GitHub Actions, an instrumental tool from the GitHub repositories ecosystem. GitHub Actions allows developers to specify automated workflows triggered by changes in the repository, ensuring a swift and automated response to code modifications.

The workflow, visually articulated in Figure 6.2, embodies a sequence of meticulously orchestrated steps, each contributing to the seamless deployment of quantum services. This process starts with the initiation detailed in Figure 6.1 *(Step 1 and 2)* and unfolds as follows:

- **Step 3: Developer commitment.** The manual intervention of developers concludes with a dedicated commit to the repository, serving as the pivotal trigger for the subsequent automated generation and deployment of quantum services.
- **Step 4: Repository specification verification.** A critical checkpoint ensues to verify the correct formatting of the repository specification. This validation is meticulously executed through the generation of services code, facilitated by the modified OpenAPI Code Generator.
- **Step 5: Code generation validation.** Ensuring the generation of code, the workflow progresses to validate the correctness of the generated code, a crucial precursor to the subsequent deployment steps.
- **Step 6: Automated deployment initialization.** With validated code in place, the workflow seamlessly transitions to the automatic deployment phase. This pivotal step commences with

Figure 6.2: Overview of the automatic quantum services deployment workflow.

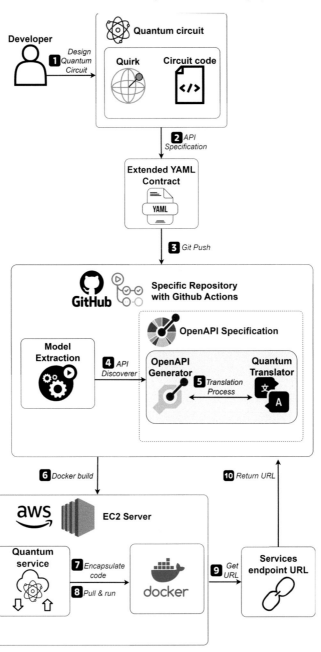

the submission of a meticulously configured request to the deployment API residing on an AWS server.

- **Step 7: Deployment request processing.** The server, responsive to the GitHub Actions call, adeptly processes the deployment request. This involves the generation and encapsulation of the code within a container.
- **Step 8: Container deployment and exposure.** The deployment unfolds with the seamless exposure of the container on the first available free port. This step is quintessential for ensuring the accessibility of the quantum services.
- **Steps 9 and 10: Quantum services availability.** Upon completion, the server furnishes the developer with the URL where the generated quantum services are hosted. This tangible outcome serves as the culmination of the workflow.

The implementation of this CD workflow is encapsulated within the repository.[22] This proposition aspires to enhance the accessibility of quantum computing by providing a tool for the seamless automatic generation and deployment of quantum services. By ushering in automation to the deployment process, our tool endeavors to bridge the gap between quantum and classical computing paradigms.

---

[22] https://github.com/javierrome236/quantumDeployment

7

Quality Aspects on Quantum Software Development

> "Quantum physics has gossip proof laws. When we look, it breaks the system, sounding the alarm if there are spies."
>
> Prof. Peter Shor

Ana Díaz Muñoz, Moisés Rodríguez, Monje, Manuel Ángel Serrano, Macario Polo, José Antonio Cruz-Lemus, and Ignacio García-Rodríguez de Guzmán
Universidad de Castilla-La Mancha, Alarcos Research Group, Spain

Quantum computing harnesses the principles of quantum mechanics for data representation and processing. This paradigm is poised to offer exponential acceleration in solving certain problems when juxtaposed with classical computing [106], particularly excelling in domains requiring extensive parallel computation and in simulating quantum phenomena, as seen in chemistry or material science [107].

As an emerging technology, the industry is rapidly outpacing advancements in quantum software engineering (QSE) in its efforts to adopt quantum computing [4]. This raises concerns since QSE is integral to the success of QC, and we must adapt and devise new processes, methods, techniques, practices, and principles from traditional software engineering for the creation of quantum software [7]. Consequently, it is critical to pay special attention to cross-cutting processes like quality management. Recent studies have pinpointed priority areas in QSE needing development [48], and there are multiple endeavors to apply the principles and practices of software engineering in these areas, such as analysis [108], design [34], maintenance [35], and quality management [109]. In particular, this chapter focuses on two of the most important backbones in software quality: software testing and quality software measurement.

On the one hand, despite progress across all previous phases of the quantum software lifecycle, testing in the latter stages remains the most effective method to ensure software quality [110]. Moreover, since human intuition and programmers' expertise are not attuned to quantum mechanics, quantum programming is anticipated to be more error-prone than classical programming, implying that programmers are likely to make a significantly higher number of mistakes when developing quantum applications [111] [112]. This, coupled with the verification challenges posed by the intrinsic characteristics of quantum computers, such as superposition and entanglement, necessitates novel systematic methods for the verification of quantum programs. Therefore, quantum software testing engineering emerges as a pertinent field of study with many topics yet to be addressed [113], including the evaluation and redefinition of fundamental engineering test concepts, like use cases, test suites, and unit tests.

So, regarding testing, we tackle the definition of quantum test cases and introduce a technique for implementing these cases through a testing circuit that incorporates inputs, expected outputs, the circuit under test (CuT), and an evaluation mechanism, as well as the process for executing a test suite with this circuit. We also include a small case study to show the new concepts that have been proposed: (i) the quantum test case, (ii) the QTC, as a quantum test circuit, which embeds the CuT in a structure able to manage the input data and expected result, and (iii) the process followed to generate and execute the test suite. As stated in the corresponding section, this proposal deals with the deterministic quantum circuit, in which the output is a specific value. Quantum circuits providing a probabilistic distribution as a result requires different testing techniques, such as property-based ones.

On the other hand, quantum software quality emerges as a crucial pillar in the development and long-term success of this technology. The increasing complexity and potential of quantum systems demand a rigorous and methodological approach to ensure that software products not only meet their initial specifications, but are also maintainable, scalable, and, above all, analyzable. In this context, we have made significant contributions to address these needs, which are presented throughout this chapter.

One of our main contributions is the development of an evaluation model designed specifically for the analyzability of quantum software. This model includes a detailed set of properties and computational methods that enable a comprehensive evaluation of the critical aspects that affect the quality and understandability of quantum software. Throughout the chapter, we present this model in detail, along with concrete examples of measurements applied to quantum circuits. These examples illustrate the applicability and relevance of the model. In addition, we have developed an evaluation environment composed of several automated tools, which facilitates the efficient measurement and evaluation of quantum software. This environment allows developers and researchers to collect quality data in a systematic way, which is essential for software validation and continuous improvement. One of the most outstanding features of our evaluation environment is the integration with the Power BI tool, which offers advanced capabilities for data analysis and reporting. Thanks to this integration, users can transform collected data into analyzable and valuable information, thus facilitating evidence-based decision-making regarding the quality and performance of quantum software.

7.1 State of the art

7.1.1 Proposals on quantum software testing

Up to now, quantum software testing has been an immature field of study. Despite this, there is a body of work in the literature that addresses quantum software testing by adapting classical testing methods. There are currently three main groups of approaches [114]:

- Probabilistic testing: Some papers address this "uncertainty tracking" [115] by estimating the failure probability, while others use statistically based assertions to make the detection.

- Verification based on formal logic: Formal verification involves the demonstration by means of logic that an algorithm is correctly implemented using a formal specification as a basis. Hoare introduced a set of logical rules that allow reasoning about the correctness of software [116], which has been the basis for a wide variety of testing approaches, including some aimed at quantum software verification [117][118].

- Applications of reversibility to testing: The reversibility of circuits is based on the conservation of energy and, thus, of information [119]. This implies some interesting features from a verification perspective, such as significantly simplifying the test suite generation problem [120].

7.1.2 Proposals on quantum software quality

Quantum computing is currently emerging as a revolutionary force in multiple fields, with its impact on areas such as artificial intelligence and medicine standing out. This technology promises solutions to problems that until now were unapproachable for classical computing. However, the exponential growth of its use brings with it a critical challenge: ensuring the quality of quantum software [7]. In this context, the importance of developing high-quality software becomes a paramount goal in the field of information technology.

Quantum software quality assessment and assurance are supported by standards such as ISO/IEC 25010 [121], part of the ISO/IEC 25000 series of standards [122], which focus on the quality assessment of software products [123]. Within these standards, software maintainability stands out as a crucial aspect. Maintainability refers to the ease with which software can be modified, corrected, adapted, and improved over time. This quality encompasses important sub-characteristics such as analyzability, which determines the ease with which the software can be examined and understood.

Despite efforts to establish best practices in quantum software maintenance [124], the industry faces significant challenges. One of the most relevant is the still immature tool support and lack of adequate infrastructure to adapt, customize, automate, and configure agile practices in the development of this type of software [125]. In an agile development environment, where rapid adaptation and continuous improvement are key, static code analyses become fundamental tools. These analyses make it possible to identify areas for improvement in real time, thus ensuring more efficient and higher quality software development [102].

Classical model for software analyzability:

Quality models are composed of a set of characteristics and properties that define software quality, used for its evaluation in different contexts, adapted to the specific needs and requirements of the software in question. The ISO/IEC 25010 standard establishes a structure for evaluating the quality of software and information systems. This standard defines eight fundamental characteristics, on the basis of which the quality of a software product can be evaluated [126]. The maintainability characteristic refers to the software's ability to be easily, effectively, and efficiently modified and adapted, both to correct errors and to improve its functionality by adapting it to new requirements. The degree of software maintainability is directly linked to its analyzability.

The software that has a good level of structuring or documentation, among other properties, facilitates the understanding and modification of the system. Therefore, a good software analyzability is fundamental throughout its life cycle. The properties for the evaluation of software analyzability, such as code structuring or documentation, are designed considering all the distinctive aspects that characterize the type of software to be evaluated. The focus so far has always been on the representation of classical components as well as on the ability to perform static analysis in the evaluation environment.

Classical analyzability properties:

The set of properties that has been used for 25 years now [127] to evaluate the analyzability of a classical software product is as follows [126]:

- Non-compliance with coding rules (CR): The existence of code that does not follow established coding conventions and standards is called non-compliance. Failure to follow these conventions can complicate the understanding and maintenance of the code.
- Documentation (Doc): The totality of comments and explanations within the source code, detailing its operation, purpose, and how it is used, constitutes the documentation. Solid documentation facilitates both understanding and maintenance of the code.
- Cyclomatic complexity (CC): Evaluated based on the number of possible logical paths through the code, it determines the complexity of a program [128]. As the cyclomatic complexity increases, it becomes more complicated to understand and maintain the code.
- Package structuring (PS): The organization and grouping of files and modules into packages or directories within a software project is known as structuring. A good structuring facilitates the navigation and management of the code, improving its analyzability.
- Class structuring (CS): The arrangement of classes in a program, which includes the definition of attributes and methods within each class and their relationships, is part of class structuring. Effective class structuring simplifies class maintenance.
- Method size (MS): The number of lines of code or instructions in a program method refers to the length of the method. Excessively long methods can make the code difficult to understand and maintain.
- Duplicate code (DC): The presence of code fragments that are repeated in multiple parts of a program is called code duplication. This can lead to redundancy and complicate updating and error correction.

The evaluation method for these properties follows the same guidelines that have already been applied in languages such as Java, JavaScript, or PHP for years to evaluate conventional software products, as described in [129]. Once the values of all properties have been determined, the next step involves the calculation of the classical analyzability index. This index will be affected by one or more of the properties whose values have been calculated above.

7.2 Testing Deterministic Quantum Software

This approach will focus on the testing of deterministic quantum circuits in real quantum execution environments without the use of simulators. For this purpose, we propose the concept of quantum test case (QTC, hereafter), which consists in the definition of a test circuit, containing the circuit under test (CuT hereafter) together with a set of quantum gates operating on an auxiliary qubit array (ancilla) that helps to deliver the verdict of the QTC over a classical one-bit register. The QTC circuit is self-generating to adapt to the CuT (which has proven to be a very suitable solution to the problem of scalability of quantum circuits [130]) and then executed once for each test vector in the test suite, taking the CuT input and expected output as its inputs, and outputting a single bit representing a successful or failed test.

7.2.1 Quantum test suite and test case definition

A test suite for the verification of a CuT consists of a set of quantum test cases satisfying a given coverage criterion. We will approach the definition of a QTC by associating the component of a classical test case with its quantum counterparts. A test case consists of a set of test inputs, execution conditions, and expected results [131]. The input of a quantum circuit consists of a quantum state, which may consist of a single qubit or a register of qubits, and an optional classical register. When executing a circuit, the execution conditions include constraints related to the execution environment, such as the need for auxiliary qubits in a given initial state or the particularities of the computer on which it will be executed.

7.2.2 Quantum test case generation

The QTC (see Figure 7.1) is created as follows: first, several qubits equal to the size of the CuT input are placed, followed by two quantum registers with the size of the corresponding outputs of the circuit. The first set represents the expected value. The qubits in the next register called the "check" register are set to $|0\rangle$. These qubits will contain the result of the comparison between the CuT output and the qubits representing the expected result. Finally, we need a qubit and a classical bit to deliver the verdict. The first transformation placed is the CuT on the first register.

Figure 7.1: Test circuit for a CuT with two inputs and one output.

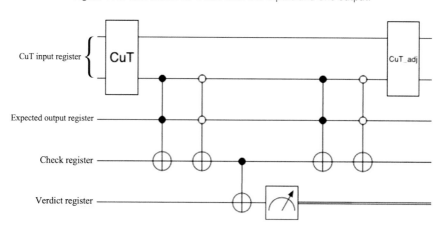

Then, a pair of Toffoli gates, one with regular checks and one with inverted checks, are placed to compare each of the CuT outputs with the respective "expected-outcome" qubit, and the result of the comparison is placed in the respective "check" qubit pointing to it. In this way, if the output 0 and the expected 0 are equal, the check 0 is set to "1" and the other to "0," and so on. After this step, a multi-controlled X-rotation with checks in each qubit of the "check" register targets the verdict qubit, which is subsequently negated and measured by outputting the result in the classical verdict bit. At this point, the classic bit will be set to "0" if the "expected" register is equal to the CuT output, and to "1" otherwise. Finally, the calculation must be reversed by reflecting the Toffoli gates and applying the adjoin version of the CuT.

7.3 Application Example

7.3.1 Quantum full adder

At this point, we have presented the concepts of quantum test suite and quantum test case, and briefly introduced the composition and working of the QTC. To illustrate the next sections, where QTC generation and execution processes are explained, we will present a toy example to facilitate the understandability of the approach. The selected CuT for the toy example is a very simple, yet functional, circuit: the quantum implementation of a 2-bit

Figure 7.2: Test circuit for a CuT with two inputs and one output.

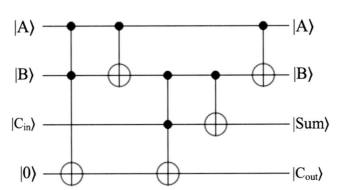

Figure 7.3: Quantum full adder test suite.

	A	B	Cin	S	Cout
Test case 0	0	0	0	0	0
Test case 1	0	0	1	1	0
Test case 2	0	1	0	1	0
Test case 3	0	1	1	0	1
Test case 4	1	0	0	1	0
Test case 5	1	0	1	0	1
Test case 6	1	1	0	0	1
Test case 7	1	1	1	1	1

full adder. Figure 7.2 depicts the circuit, while Figure 7.3 presents its expected behavior described as a set of test cases.

The first two qubits ($|A\rangle$, $|B\rangle$) represent the bits to be added, and the third one represents the carry in ($|Cin\rangle$). Due to the nature of the circuit, the fourth qubit's input is always $|0\rangle$, as seen in Figure 7.2. Regarding the CuT's output, the two first qubits remain with the same value as the computation is reverted on them. The third qubit contains the result of the add (identified as |Sumâ§), and the fourth qubit represents the carry out ($|Cout\rangle$). Then, this circuit has three significant input qubits (input register containing A, B, and $|Cin\rangle$), with only two significant outputs (output register containing Sum and $|Cout\rangle$). These are the qubits that will be considered in the test cases. Due to the reduced size of the test vectors, it is reasonable to use the full truth table, depicted in Figure 7.3, as a test suite. In the context of this toy example, the verification is therefore exhaustive.

7.3.2 Generation and execution of the test circuit

Following the aforementioned generation process, the test circuit is shown in Figure 7.4.

Figure 7.4: Test circuit for a quantum full adder.

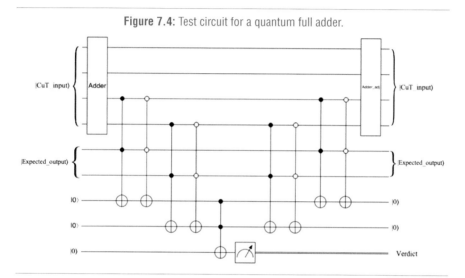

7.3.3 Execution of the toy example

Following the toy example of the quantum adder, it is now possible to exemplify the effect of the execution of the test cases designed for the quantum adder. Figure 7.3 shows a table that summarizes the eight test possible test cases of the test suite for the CuT. On the left side of the table, three bits of input data (initial states of the input qubits) are specified, while on the right side of the table, the corresponding expected output is depicted by using two bits (corresponding to the states of the output qubits where the result holds).

To automate the process, we have developed a script in Qiskit (see Figure 7.5) to automate the test suite execution [132]. After the execution, the test suite is successfully passed, retrieving the console output depicted in Figure 7.6.

Figure 7.5: Pseudocode for QTCC generation and execution.

```
1    test_process(CuT, output_indexes, test_suite, n_shots):
2
3        failed_tests = {0}
4        ∀ test_case ∈ test_suite:
5            input = test_case[input_data]
6            expected_result = test_case[output_data]
7            QTC = generate QTC(CuT, output_indexes, input,
8                expected_result)
9            verdict = executeQTC(QTC, shots)
10           if(verdict):
11               failed_tests = failed_tests ∪ test_case
12       return failed_tests
```

Figure 7.6: Output of the execution of the quantum test cases.

```
test suite =
(((0,0,0), (0,0)), ((0,0,1), (1,0)), ((0,1,0), (1,0)), ((0,1,1), (0,1)), ((1,0,0),
(1,0)), ((1,0,1), (0,1)), ((1,1,0), (0,1)), ((1,1,1), (1,1)))

`Test suite passed: all tests successful`
```

The previous is an ideal situation when all the tests are passed by the QTCC, but to check the behavior of the QTC when there exist test cases that do not succeed, three negative test cases have been introduced (see Figure 7.7) to verify that the test process is robust regarding to false positives and false negatives.

Figure 7.7: Negative test cases.

	A	B	C_{in}	S	C_{in}
Test case 0	0	0	0	1	0
Test case 2	0	1	0	1	1
Test case 4	1	0	0	0	0

Figure 7.8 shows the console output after the execution of the script. The script reveals that the test suite is not successful, with three failing test cases.

Figure 7.8: Console output after the bugged test suite execution.

```
test suite =
(((0,0,0), (0,0)), ((0,0,1), (1,0)), ((0,1,0), (1,0)), ((0,1,1), (0,1)), ((1,0,0),
(1,0)), ((1,0,1), (0,1)), ((1,1,0), (0,1)), ((1,1,1), (1,1)))

`Test suite passed: all tests successful`
```

7.4 Quantum Software Quality

7.4.1 Analyzability properties for quantum software

The quality properties that influence the analysis capability of quantum software are as follows:

- Coding rule (CR) non-compliance: The existence of code that does not comply with established conventions and standards for quantum programming. Since there is currently no established standard for quantum code coding rules, this property is not yet taken into account when assessing the analyzability of quantum software.
- Circuit width (CW): The number of cubits required to represent and manipulate the information in a quantum circuit. A wider circuit may require more resources and be more complicated to analyze.
- Circuit depth (CD): The number of layers that make up a quantum circuit. Greater depth can increase the complexity of the circuit and thus make it more difficult to understand.
- Circuit gate complexity (CCG): Evaluates the number and type of quantum gates used in a circuit. The difficulty of understanding and modifying the circuit increases with more complex gates applied on a larger number of cubits.
- Conditional instructions (CI): The operations performed on a quantum circuit based on the results of previous measurements on the cubits. This adds complexity and may require more meticulous and detailed analysis to understand the circuit.
- Quantum cyclomatic complexity (QCC): The complexity of a quantum program in terms of the number of possible logic paths through the quantum code [128]. Higher cyclomatic complexity may indicate a circuit that is more difficult to analyze.
- Measurement operations (MO): Instructions that allow information about the state of one or more cubits to be extracted. They are critical at specific points because they represent the interaction between the states of the cubits and the bits; an inappropriate choice of measurement points may affect the analyzability of the algorithm.
- Initialization and reset operations (IRO): The operations that prepare the initial state of the cubits prior to circuit execution and those that reset them to a known state after execution. Understanding how cubits are set and reset can complicate circuit understanding.
- Auxiliary cubits (AQ): The additional cubits to perform certain operations in a circuit. These auxiliary cubits directly influence the complexity of the algorithm and require additional analysis to understand how they affect the behavior of the circuit.

Analogous to the evaluation performed with classical properties, quantum properties are evaluated using the profile function. These profile functions are interpreted similarly and are based on AQCLab's experience in assessing maintainability [129].

7.4.2 Analyzability metrics for quantum software

In this section, we examine the computational procedures established for the set of specific metrics designed to quantify and evaluate the various properties related to analysis capability in quantum software.

The computational methods constitute the procedures and algorithms used to quantitatively measure the various aspects of analysis capability; they provide a quantitative basis for evaluating and comparing the software's suitability to be effectively analyzed and understood. Metrics, on the other hand, are numerical indicators derived from these methods, providing specific measures of analysis properties. With these metrics, it is possible to obtain an objective and quantifiable understanding of the analysis capability of quantum software, identifying areas that may require adjustment or improvement.

It is important to note that the metrics established for the evaluation of quantum software properties (see Table 7.1) are based on the work done by Cruz-Lemus et al. [133]. In the study by Díaz et al. [134], an initial version of the metrics for evaluating the analysis capability of hybrid (classical-quantum) systems was presented, which have been refined and improved through various evaluations performed on real products during this work.

This work focuses on the properties of the quantum part. An example of a calculation procedure used to obtain the values reflecting the quality of the quantum software through the evaluation of the different quantum properties for analyzability is detailed below.

Calculation of the circuit width:

The quality property called "circuit width" in the context of quantum software refers to the number of initialized cubits in a quantum circuit. An example of calculating the width of a quantum circuit is shown in Figure 7.9, where a value of 4 is obtained for its width.

To evaluate this property on the quantum circuit, levels are defined and a profile function is used to indicate the maximum accepted number of circuits for each quality level. Once the various circuits have been classified according to the number of cubits they contain, their distribution is evaluated using base metrics. These metrics are divided into three levels, with level 3 being the least critical and level 1 the most significant:

- NC_CW1: Number of circuits with a circuit width of level 1.
- NC_CW2: Number of circuits with a circuit width of level 2.

Table 7.1: Definition of quantum metrics for analyzability.

Property	Acronym	Base metrics	Derived metrics
Circuit width	CW	NC_CW1 NC_CW2 NC_CW3 NCIR	DC_CW1 DC_CW2 DC_CW3
Circuit depth	CD	NC_CD1 NC_CD2 NC_CD3 NCIR	DC_CD1 DC_CD2 DC_CD3
Complexity of circuit gates	CCG	NG_CG1 NG_CG2 NG_CG3 NG	DG_CG1 DG_CG2 DG_CG3
Conditional instructions	CI	NC_CI1 NC_CI2 NC_CI3 NCIR	DC_CI1 DC_CI2 DC_CI3
Quantum cyclomatic complexity	QCC	NC_QCC1 NC_QCC2 NC_QCC3 NCIR	DC_QCC1 DC_QCC2 DC_QCC3
Measurement operations	MO	NC_MO1 NC_MO2 NC_MO3 NCIR	DC_MO1 DC_MO2 DC_MO3
Initialize and reset operations	IRO	NC_IRO1 NC_IRO2 NC_IRO3 NCIR	DC_IRO1 DC_IRO2 DC_IRO3
Auxiliary qubits	AQ	N_AQ NQ	D_AQ

- NC_CW3: Number of circuits with a circuit width of level 3.
- NCIR: Total number of circuits.

The calculation of these base metrics, defined for the circuit width property, is performed based on the thresholds specified in Table 7.2, which have been established based on the experience accumulated in various measurements. These thresholds are used to assign quality levels to the circuit width taking into account its analyzability, where level 1 indicates a poor width, level 2 a fair width, and level 3 a good width.

From these base metrics, the following derivative metrics are calculated:

- DC_CW1: Density of circuits with level 1 circuit width.
- DC_CW2: Density of circuits with level 2 circuit width.

Figure 7.9: Representation of the circuit width.

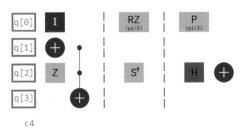

c4

Table 7.2: Levels for circuit width evaluation.

Ranges

Levels				Quality Levels
	1	>15	Bad circuit width	
	2	9-15	Fair circuit width	
	3	1-8	Good circuit width	

| • DC_CW3: Density of circuits with level 3 circuit width.

These derived metrics are obtained by dividing the number of circuits at each level by the total number of circuits evaluated. Eqn (7.1) shows how the derived circuit density metric is calculated with level 1 circuit width. The other derived metrics used in the evaluation of this property are calculated in an analogous manner.

$$DC\_CW1 = \frac{NC\_CW1}{NCIR}. \tag{7.1}$$

Once these three densities are obtained, a normalized quality value for the property is determined using the profile function. In the profile function for the circuit width, the following ranges are defined, as shown in Table 7.3. For

Table 7.3: Levels and ranges for circuit width evaluation

Levels

Ranges		1	2	Quality Levels
	0	-	-	0
	1	20	40	(0-33)
	2	15	30	[33-66)
	3	10	20	[66-100)
	4	7	15	100

each quality level, the maximum accepted threshold of circuit density is set. It should be noted that the table does not include the most desirable width level, which corresponds to a good circuit width.

7.4.3 Environment for the evaluation of the analyzability of quantum software

This section presents the technological environment developed and designed to measure, evaluate, and visualize the results of quantum software analyzability.

A representation of the architecture of the different technologies is provided in Figure 7.10. This environment is composed of three tools: the measurement tool, the evaluation tool, and the data query and analysis tool. The modular and well-defined architecture of the environment facilitates a smooth interaction between these tools, allowing an efficient evaluation of the analysis capability of quantum software. In addition, the choice of PostgreSQL as the central point of storage and communication between the tools ensures data integrity and availability throughout the entire evaluation process. Primarily, we have chosen to use SonarQube[23] as the development environment for the measurement component, based on two key advantages. First, its ability to support a wide range of programming languages stands out. Secondly, the flexibility offered by SonarQube in incorporating custom extensions or plugins is fundamental. This feature gives us the ability to adjust the tool to the specific needs of quantum systems. We have created a "quantum plugin" that integrates the proposed metrics to evaluate the analyzability of quantum software. Thanks to this functionality, we can tailor the platform metrics in a customized way to meet the specific requirements of our project.

The most essential part in the evaluation of quantum software is the evaluation tool, which consists of two fundamental components. First, there is an XML file containing the defined properties, metrics, calculation methods, and quality levels. In addition, a program developed in Python has been created that automates the application of the XML information to the results obtained during the measurement of the source code. This Python program is mainly responsible for interpreting and processing the measurement data. It compares the values obtained for the metrics with the ranges and quality levels established in the XML, which represents the model. It also calculates the level of analyzability for the quantum software. In parallel, the evaluation tool exports the results to the same PostgreSQL database to consolidate the information resulting from the evaluation.

---

[23]https://www.sonarsource.com/products/sonarqube/

Figure 7.10: Architecture of the technological environment for assessing analyzability.

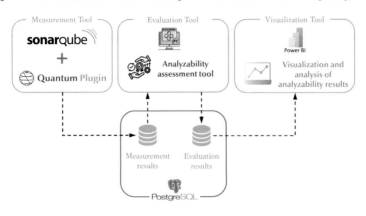

Finally, the data examination and exploration utility plays a fundamental role in extracting the evaluation results from the PostgreSQL database. This tool enables the execution of queries and data analysis efficiently, providing meaningful data on the analyzability of the quantum software to the evaluation manager or software auditor.

7.5 Conclusion

Quantum computing is experiencing exponential growth in terms of its development. However, it is not only hardware that will be decisive for the application of this paradigm to (so far unsolvable) problems that will bring value to our society. Quantum software is the differentiating element that, by harnessing the power of this new paradigm, will make it possible to address all the challenges for which quantum computing is necessary. However, techniques and tools are required to facilitate the development of quality quantum software in a sustainable way, avoiding falling into a new software crisis.

On the one hand, this chapter presents some advances made in the field of quantum software testing. Classically, testing is one of the crucial processes that ensure error-free software development. However, the physical properties on which quantum software is based mean that its testing is not the same as that of classical software. While it is possible to take inspiration from some of the classical testing techniques, quantum software needs to rethink the testing phase, for which it is necessary not only to redefine many of its concepts but also to propose new techniques. Thus, one of the approaches being developed, that of testing quantum circuits with deterministic behavior, is briefly presented. This approach makes it possible to redefine concepts such as the quantum test suite, and the quantum test case, and to create artifacts by means of which to begin testing quantum software in the form of circuits.

On the other hand, this chapter presents the properties for measuring and evaluating the analyzability of quantum software, also reviewing the properties for the classical part. A technological environment capable of providing an analyzability value for a quantum product following the established guidelines has been created. Additional tests are currently being carried out by software auditors to ensure the correct functioning and use of the environment as a whole. It is important to note that the measurement tool has already been employed during previous research, such as that shown in [91], where it was used to measure metrics in 16 quantum algorithms, such as Shor's algorithm [135] or Grover's algorithm [16]. This work contributed to the identification of improvements in the production and implementation of specific quantum services. As for measurement in Sonar, the goal is to integrate it into a DevOps environment to perform measurements automatically. In the long term, this will involve incorporating other tools from the environment into this future pipeline.

This work not only lays the groundwork for more comprehensive and accurate quality assessments in the future but also proposes the incorporation of new development ideas. One such idea is the expansion of the evaluation environment to address other crucial features of quantum software quality.

Acknowledgments

This work has been carried out in the context of the QSERV-UCLM project (PID2021-124054OB-C32) funded by the Spanish Ministry of Science and Innovation (MICINN).

8

Conclusions and Future Directions

"Science cannot solve the
ultimate mystery of nature.
And that is because, in the
last analysis, we ourselves
are part of nature and
therefore part of the
mystery that we are trying
to solve."

Nobel laureate Max Planck

8.1 Conclusions

The field of quantum computing is undergoing a rapid and dynamic
evolution, showcasing the potential to revolutionize problem-solving across
diverse domains. This transformative journey is characterized by the ongoing
exploration of both foundational principles and practical applications of
quantum computing. Researchers and practitioners are delving into the
intricate world of quantum mechanics, harnessing phenomena such as
superposition and entanglement to develop novel quantum algorithms.
Simultaneously, practical applications are being pursued, ranging from
optimization problems and cryptography to machine learning and materials
science. This multidimensional exploration is expanding our understanding
of quantum computing's capabilities and paving the way for unprecedented

advancements that hold the promise of reshaping the landscape of computational possibilities in profound ways. As this evolution continues, the integration of quantum computing into real-world scenarios is becoming increasingly tangible, marking a transformative era in the realm of information processing.

Parallel to the remarkable scientific advances in quantum computing, commercial growth is occurring in this field. Numerous large computer companies have ventured into the development of their quantum computers, making them available to users through a variety of models, often adopting a pay-per-use approach. This commercialization of quantum computing is not only making this cutting-edge technology more accessible but is also fostering a competitive and innovative market. At the same time, engineers have been instrumental in the design and implementation of a multitude of quantum programming languages, simulators, and toolkits. These tools play a crucial role in enabling researchers, developers, and companies to engage in quantum computing, experiment with algorithms, and explore the potential applications of this revolutionary technology. This vibrant ecosystem is laying the foundation for the field of quantum software and services, with a range of possibilities for industries ranging from finance to healthcare.

The purpose of this book is to provide a comprehensive exploration of quantum computing, covering from its foundational principles to its practical applications in the development of quantum services. It begins with a review of the fundamental aspects of quantum computing, explaining concepts such as qubits, superposition and entanglement, targeting readers with varying degrees of familiarity with the subject.

Beyond the basic concepts, the book goes on to explore some of the challenges faced by quantum software developers in the current landscape. To this end, it addresses issues related to low-level abstractions and the absence of integration, deployment, and quality assurance mechanisms in quantum software engineering. To this end, we explore the principles of service-oriented computing as they are applied to the realm of quantum computing. This exploration reveals architectural patterns that are specifically customized to the unique characteristics and requirements of quantum computing systems. By identifying and elucidating these architectural patterns, we aim to provide a structured framework that can effectively harness the potential of quantum computing in a service-oriented context.

Moreover, our focus extends to the critical considerations of standardization and accessibility within the quantum computing domain. Standardization efforts are pivotal in establishing a common ground for interoperability and collaboration, enabling the seamless integration of quantum services into existing computational landscapes. Concurrently, addressing accessibility concerns ensures that the benefits of quantum computing are made available to a broader audience, fostering inclusivity and democratizing access to this transformative technology.

Through this comprehensive examination of service-oriented computing principles in the context of quantum computing, we aim to contribute to the development of a robust and accessible quantum computing ecosystem, paving the way for innovative applications and widespread adoption of quantum technologies.

8.2 Vision for the Future in Quantum Computing as a Service

The transformative potential inherent in quantum technology goes beyond the transformative impact witnessed during the Internet era. This assertion underscores the profound and disruptive nature of quantum computing, hinting at the possibility of far-reaching implications that could radically reshape numerous sectors across industries. The unparalleled computational power offered by quantum computers has the potential to revolutionize several fields ushering in a new era of technological capabilities. However, the realization of this transformative potential is contingent upon making quantum technology more accessible to computing professionals. This accessibility extends beyond mere training and education, and it involves standardizing access to all available quantum computing resources. Establishing common protocols and languages can streamline the integration of quantum computing into existing workflows, making it more approachable.

Furthermore, fostering interdisciplinary collaborations is crucial for unlocking the full potential of quantum computing. By bringing together experts from diverse fields, including quantum physicists, computer scientists, mathematicians, and domain-specific professionals, we can collectively explore and exploit the multifaceted applications of quantum technology. This collaborative approach not only accelerates innovation but also ensures that the benefits of quantum computing are realized across a spectrum of industries, contributing to the broader advancement of scientific knowledge and technological capabilities. In essence, democratizing access, standardizing protocols, and encouraging interdisciplinary collaboration are pivotal steps toward shaping a future where quantum computing becomes an integral and accessible component of the technological landscape.

In conclusion, this book reflects the dynamic and rapidly evolving nature of quantum computing, supported by significant research and development efforts, funding, and a vision for the future. It also emphasizes the accessibility of quantum computing knowledge to a diverse audience, highlighting its potential impact on various industries and society as a whole.

Authors' Guide to Quantum Computing Slang

Quantum computing: A paradigm of computing that utilizes the principles of quantum mechanics, particularly the phenomena of superposition and entanglement, to process information. Unlike classical computers that use bits, quantum computers use qubits to perform complex calculations more efficiently for certain types of problems.

Quantum computer: A machine that uses the properties of quantum physics to store data and perform computations.

Quantum simulator: A classical computing system or software designed to simulate the behavior of a quantum computer. Quantum simulators allow researchers and developers to test and debug quantum algorithms without the need for access to actual quantum hardware.

Quantum cloud: Cloud-based services that provide access to quantum computers and simulators over the internet.

Hybrid classical-quantum system: A computational model or architecture that combines classical computing elements with quantum computing elements. It aims to leverage the strengths of both classical and quantum computation, allowing for the development of applications that benefit from the parallelism and unique properties of quantum computing while integrating with classical systems.

Qubit: The fundamental unit of quantum information, analogous to a classical bit but with the ability to exist in multiple states simultaneously.

Superposition: A fundamental principle of quantum mechanics where a quantum system, such as a qubit, can exist in multiple states at the same time.

Entanglement: A phenomenon where qubits become correlated and the state of one qubit instantaneously influences the state of another, regardless of the distance between them.

Quantum state: The complete description of the physical and mathematical properties of a quantum system. It includes information about the probabilities of different outcomes when measurements are made on the system.

Bell state: A specific entangled quantum state of two qubits that are maximally entangled.

Measurement: It is the act of observing a quantum state. This observation will produce classical information, such as a bit. It is important to note that this measurement process will change the quantum state.

Quantum teleportation: A quantum communication process by which the state of a qubit is transmitted from one location to another, without the physical transfer of the qubit itself. It relies on the principles of entanglement and quantum superposition to achieve the transmission of quantum information.

Quantum supremacy: The theoretical point at which a quantum computer can perform tasks that are practically impossible for classical computers to execute within a reasonable time frame.

Decoherence: The loss of quantum coherence, where a quantum system loses its ability to exist in multiple states and settles into a single state due to external factors.

Noisy intermediate-scale quantum (NISQ): Quantum computers that are small and error-prone but still valuable for specific computational tasks.

Quantum cryptography: It is a type of cryptography that uses the principles of quantum physics to create a message that is indecipherable to all but the quantum.

Quantum error correction: Techniques and algorithms used to mitigate errors in quantum computations caused by environmental factors, noise, and imperfections in quantum hardware.

Quantum circuit: A sequence of quantum gates and operations that manipulate qubits to perform a specific quantum computation.

Quantum annealing: A quantum computing approach designed for optimization problems, utilizing principles of quantum mechanics to find the global minimum of a given objective function.

Braket: Amazon Braket is a fully managed quantum computing service provided by Amazon Web Services (AWS). It allows users to build, test, and run quantum algorithms on different quantum processors and simulators.

Cirq: A quantum programming framework developed by Google for designing, simulating, and running quantum circuits on Google's quantum processors.

Qiskit: An open-source quantum computing software development framework by IBM, allowing users to write quantum circuits using Python.

Quantum algorithm: A set of instructions designed for execution on a quantum computer to solve a specific problem more efficiently than classical algorithms. Quantum algorithms often leverage the principles of superposition and entanglement to achieve computational speedup.

Grover's algorithm: A quantum algorithm for searching unsorted databases exponentially faster than classical algorithms.

Shor's algorithm: A quantum algorithm for integer factorization that threatens the security of widely used classical cryptographic schemes.

Quantum walk: A quantum analogue to classical random walks, often used in quantum algorithms for searching and graph-related problems.

Bloch sphere: It refers to the Swiss physicist Felix Bloch and is a geometric representation of the state space of a two-level quantum system.

Quantum gates: The quantum counterparts to classical logic gates, which are used in quantum circuits to perform operations with qubits.

Hadamard gate: A quantum gate that creates a superposition of states, often used in quantum algorithms for its transformative properties.

Schrödinger's cat: It is a thought experiment described as a paradox by the physicist of the same name. A cat in a box can be alive or dead, but we do not know it until we open the box, because at that moment the function collapses and takes a certain value.

Bibliography

[1] E. R. MacQuarrie, C. Simon, S. Simmons, E. Maine, The emerging commercial landscape of quantum computing, Nature Reviews Physics 2 (11) (2020) 596–598. doi:10.1038/s42254-020-00247-5.

[2] M. J. Klein, Max planck and the beginnings of the quantum theory, Archive for History of Exact Sciences 1 (5) (1961) 459–479. doi:10.1007/BF00327765.

[3] R. P. Feynman, et al., Simulating physics with computers, Int. j. Theor. phys 21 (6/7) (2018). doi:10.1007/BF02650179.

[4] J. Zhao, Quantum Software Engineering: Landscapes and Horizons, Arxiv.ArXiv: 2007.07047 (jul 2020). arXiv:2007.07047.

[5] A. M. Chanu, V. Kumar, Quantum supremacy: How far along are we on the journey?, in: 2021 Asian Conference on Innovation in Technology (ASIANCON), IEEE, 2021, pp. 1–8. doi:10.1109/ASIANCON51346.2021.9544619.

[6] A. Bayerstadler, G. Becquin, J. Binder, T. Botter, H. Ehm, T. Ehmer, M. Erdmann, N. Gaus, P. Harbach, M. Hess, et al., Industry quantum computing applications, EPJ Quantum Technology 8 (1) (2021) 25. doi:10.1140/epjqt/s40507-021-00114-x.

[7] M. Piattini, G. Peterssen, R. Pérez-Castillo, J. L. Hevia, M. A. Serrano, G. Hernández, I. G. R. de Guzmán, et al., The talavera manifesto for quantum software engineering and programming, in: Short Papers Proceedings of the 1st International Workshop on the QuANtum SoftWare Engineering & pRogramming, Talavera de la Reina, Spain, 2020, Vol. 2561 of CEUR Workshop Proceedings, CEUR-WS.org, 2020, pp. 1–5. URL http://ceur-ws.org/Vol-2561/paper0.pdf

[8] J. D. Hidary, Dirac Notation, Quantum Computing: An Applied Approach (2021) 377–381doi:10.1007/978-3-030-83274-2_14.

[9]   D. Bouwmeester, A. Zeilinger, The physics of quantum information: basic concepts, in: The physics of quantum information: quantum cryptography, quantum teleportation, quantum computation, Springer, 2000, pp. 1–14. doi:10.1007/978-3-662-04209-0_1.

[10] E. Schrödinger, The present status of quantum mechanics, Die Naturwissenschaften 23 (48) (1935) 1–26. URL https://homepages.dias.ie/dorlas/Papers/QMSTATUS.pdf

[11] R. Horodecki, P. Horodecki, M. Horodecki, K. Horodecki, Quantum entanglement, Reviews of modern physics 81 (2) (2009) 865. doi:10.1103/RevModPhys.81.865.

[12] V. Mavroeidis, K. Vishi, M. D. Zych, A. Jøsang, The impact of quantum computing on present cryptography, arXiv preprint (2018). doi:10.48550/arXiv.1804.00200.

[13] W. K. Wootters, W. H. Zurek, A single quantum cannot be cloned, Nature 299 (5886) (1982) 802–803. doi:10.1038/299802a0.

[14] L. M. Kohnfelder, Towards a practical public-key cryptosystem., Ph.D. thesis, Massachusetts Institute of Technology (1978). doi:1721.1/15993.

[15] P. W. Shor, Polynomial-time algorithms for prime factorization and discrete logarithms on a quantum computer, SIAM review 41 (2) (1999) 303–332. doi:10.1137/S0036144598347011.

[16] L. K. Grover, A fast quantum mechanical algorithm for database search, in: Proceedings of the twenty-eighth annual ACM symposium on Theory of computing, 1996, pp. 212–219. doi:10.48550/arXiv.quant-ph/9605043.

[17] D. Collins, K. W. Kim, W. C. Holton, Deutsch-jozsa algorithm as a test of quantum computation, Physical Review A - Atomic, Molecular, and Optical Physics 58 (1998) 1633–1636. doi:10.1103/PhysRevA.58.R1633.

[18] D. R. Simon, On the power of quantum computation, SIAM journal on computing 26 (5) (1997) 1474–1483. doi:10.1137/S009753979629863.

[19] F. Leymann, J. Barzen, M. Falkenthal, D. Vietz, B. Weder, K. Wild, Quantum in the cloud: application potentials and research opportunities, arXiv preprint arXiv:2003.06256 (2020). doi:10.48550/arXiv.2003.06256.

[20] K. Wild, U. Breitenbucher, L. Harzenetter, F. Leymann, D. Vietz, M. Zimmermann, TOSCA4QC: Two Modeling Styles for TOSCA to Automate the Deployment and Orchestration of Quantum Applications, Proceedings - 2020 IEEE 24th International Enterprise Distributed Object Computing Conference, EDOC (2020) 125–134. doi:10.1109/EDOC49727.2020.00024.

[21] D. Cuomo, M. Caleffi, A. S. Cacciapuoti, Towards a Distributed Quantum Computing Ecosystem, IET Quantum Communication 1 (1) (2020) 3–8. arXiv:2002.11808v2, doi:10.1049/iet-qtc.2020.0002.

[22] A. W. Cross, The ibm q experience and qiskit open-source quantum computing software, Bulletin of the American Physical Society (2018). URL https://api.semanticscholar.org/CorpusID:67150463

[23] F. Hu, B.-N. Wang, N. Wang, C. Wang, Quantum machine learning with d-wave quantum computer, Quantum Engineering 1 (2) (2019) e12. doi:10.1002/que2.12.

[24] S. Li, H. Zhang, Z. Jia, C. Zhong, C. Zhang, Z. Shan, J. Shen, M. A. Babar, Understanding and addressing quality attributes of microservices architecture: A systematic literature review, Information and Software Technology 131 (2021) 106449. doi:10.1016/j.infsof.2020.106449.

[25] D. Valencia, J. Garcia-Alonso, J. Rojo, E. Moguel, J. Berrocal, J. M. Murillo, Hybrid classical-quantum software services systems: Exploration of the rough edges, in: International Conference on the Quality of Information and Communications Technology, Springer, 2021, pp. 225–238. doi:10.1007/978-3-030-85347-1_17.

[26] T. Kennedy, Electronic computer flashes answers, may speed engineering, New York Times 15 (1946).

[27] G. L. Steele, Macaroni is better than spaghetti, ACM SIGPLAN Notices 12 (1977) 60–66. doi:10.1145/872734.806933.

[28] P. W. Shor, Scheme for reducing decoherence in quantum computer memory, Physical review A 52 (4) (1995) R2493. doi:10.1103/PhysRevA.52.R2493.

[29] J. Kelly, R. Barends, A. G. Fowler, A. Megrant, E. Jeffrey, T. C. White, D. Sank, J. Y. Mutus, B. Campbell, Y. Chen, Z. Chen, B. Chiaro, A. Dunsworth, I. C. Hoi, C. Neill, P. J. O'Malley, C. Quintana, P. Roushan, A. Vainsencher, J. Wenner, A. N. Cleland, J. M. Martinis, State preservation by repetitive error detection in a superconducting quantum circuit, Nature 2015 519:7541 519 (2015) 66–69. doi:10.1038/nature14270.

[30] C. K. Andersen, A. Remm, S. Lazar, S. Krinner, N. Lacroix, G. J. Norris, M. Gabureac, C. Eichler, A. Wallraff, Repeated quantum error detection in a surface code, Nature Physics 2020 16:8 16 (2020) 875–880. doi:10.1038/s41567-020-0920-y.

[31] M. Dyakonov, When will useful quantum computers be constructed? not in the foreseeable future, this physicist argues. here's why: The case against: Quantum computing, IEEE Spectrum 56 (2019) 24–29. doi:10.1109/MSPEC.2019.8651931.

[32] E. W. Dijkstra, The humble programmer, Communications of the ACM 15 (1972) 859–866. doi:10.1145/355604.361591.

[33] P. Mario, P. Guido, P.-C. Ricardo, Quantum computing, ACM SIGSOFT Software Engineering Notes 87 (2021) 36–41. doi:10.1145/3402127.3402131.

[34] C. A. Pérez-Delgado, H. G. Perez-Gonzalez, Towards a quantum software modeling language, Proceedings - 2020 IEEE/ACM 42nd International Conference on Software Engineering Workshops, ICSEW 2020 (2020) 442–444doi:10.1145/3387940.3392183.

[35] L. Jiménez-Navajas, R. Pérez-Castillo, M. Piattini, Reverse engineering of quantum programs toward kdm models, Communications in Computer and Information Science 1266 CCIS (2020) 249–262. doi:10.1007/978-3-030-58793-2_20.

[36] E. Moguel, J. Berrocal, J. García-Alonso, J. M. Murillo, A roadmap for quantum software engineering: Applying the lessons learned from the classics., in: Q-SET@ QCE, 2020, pp. 5–13. URL https://ceur-ws.org/Vol-2705/short1.pdf

[37] B. Heim, M. Soeken, S. Marshall, C. Granade, M. Roetteler, A. Geller, M. Troyer, K. Svore, Quantum programming languages, Nature Reviews Physics 2 (12) (2020) 709–722. doi:10.1038/s42254-020-00245-7.

[38] S. Garhwal, M. Ghorani, A. Ahmad, Quantum programming language: A systematic review of research topic and top cited languages, Archives of Computational Methods in Engineering 28 (2021) 289–310. doi:10.1007/s11831-019-09372-6.

[39] F. Leymann, Towards a pattern language for quantum algorithms, in: Quantum Technology and Optimization Problems: First International Workshop, QTOP 2019, Munich, Germany, March 18, 2019, Proceedings 1, Springer, 2019, pp. 218–230. doi:10.1007/978-3-030-14082-3_19.

[40] M. Ying, Y. Feng, Quantum loop programs, Acta Informatica 47 (2010) 221–250. doi:10.1007/s00236-010-0117-4.

[41] S. Newman, Building microservices, " O'Reilly Media, Inc.", 2021.

[42] O. Zimmermann, Microservices tenets: Agile approach to service development and deployment, Computer Science-Research and Development 32 (2017) 301–310. doi:10.1007/s00450-016-0337-0.

[43] J. Bogner, A. Zimmermann, Towards integrating microservices with adaptable enterprise architecture, in: 2016 IEEE 20th International Enterprise Distributed Object Computing Workshop (EDOCW), IEEE, 2016, pp. 1–6. doi:10.1109/EDOCW.2016.7584392.

[44] A. Sill, The design and architecture of microservices, IEEE Cloud Computing 3 (5) (2016) 76–80. doi:10.1109/MCC.2016.111.

[45] L. Chen, Microservices: architecting for continuous delivery and devops, in: 2018 IEEE International conference on software architecture (ICSA), IEEE, 2018, pp. 39–397. doi:10.1109/ICSA.2018.00013.

[46] Á. M. Aparicio-Morales, J. L. Herrera, E. Moguel, J. Berrocal, J. Garcia-Alonso, J. M. Murillo, Minimizing deployment cost of hybrid applications, in: 2023 IEEE International Conference on Quantum

Computing and Engineering (QCE), Vol. 2, IEEE, 2023, pp. 191–194. doi:10.1109/QCE57702.2023.10209.

[47] M. Rahaman, M. M. Islam, A review on progress and problems of quantum computing as a service (qcaas) in the perspective of cloud computing, Global Journal of Computer Science and Technology 15 (4) (2015).

[48] M. Piattini, G. Peterssen, R. Pérez-Castillo, Quantum computing: A new software engineering golden age, ACM SIGSOFT Software Engineering Notes 45 (3) (2021) 12–14. doi:10.1145/3402127.3402131.

[49] G. G. Guerreschi, A. Y. Matsuura, Qaoa for max-cut requires hundreds of qubits for quantum speed-up, Scientific reports 9 (1) (2019) 6903. doi:s41598-019-43176-9.

[50] J. Tilly, H. Chen, S. Cao, D. Picozzi, K. Setia, Y. Li, E. Grant, L. Wossnig, et al., The variational quantum eigensolver: a review of methods and best practices, Physics Reports 986 (2022) 1–128. doi:10.1016/j.physrep.2022.08.003.

[51] J. Rojo, D. Valencia, J. Berrocal, E. Moguel, J. Garcia-Alonso, J. M. M. Rodriguez, Trials and tribulations of developing hybrid quantum-classical microservices systems, arXiv preprint arXiv:2105.04421 (2021). doi:10.48550/arXiv.2105.04421.

[52] S. Boixo, T. Albash, F. M. Spedalieri, N. Chancellor, D. A. Lidar, Experimental signature of programmable quantum annealing, Nature communications 4 (1) (2013) 2067. doi:10.1038/ncomms3067.

[53] R. Wille, R. Van Meter, Y. Naveh, Ibmâs qiskit tool chain: Working with and developing for real quantum computers, in: 2019 Design, Automation & Test in Europe Conference & Exhibition (DATE), IEEE, 2019, pp. 1234–1240. doi:10.23919/DATE.2019.8715261.

[54] K. Brown, B. Woolf, Implementation patterns for microservices architectures, in: Proceedings of the 23rd conference on pattern languages of programs, 2016, pp. 1–35.https://hillside.net/plop/2016/papers/proceedings/papers/brown.pdf

[55] D. Valencia, E. Moguel, J. Rojo, J. Berrocal, J. Garcia-Alonso, J. M. Murillo, Quantum service-oriented architectures: From hybrid classical approaches to future stand-alone solutions, in: Quantum Software Engineering, Springer, 2022, pp. 149–166. doi:10.1007/978-3-031-05324-5_8.

[56] S. Schwichtenberg, C. Gerth, G. Engels, From open api to semantic specifications and code adapters, in: 2017 IEEE International Conference on Web Services (ICWS), IEEE, 2017, pp. 484–491. doi:10.1109/ICWS.2017.56.

[57]   B. Fitzgerald, K.-J. Stol, Continuous software engineering: A roadmap and agenda, Journal of Systems and Software 123 (2017) 176–189. doi:10.1016/j.jss.2015.06.063.

[58]   E. Moguel, J. Garcia-Alonso, M. Haghparast, J. M. Murillo, Quantum microservices development and deployment, arXiv preprint arXiv:2309.11926 (2023). doi:10.48550/arXiv.2309.11926.

[59]   J. Bonilla, E. Moguel, J. García-Alonso, C. Canal, Integration of classical and quantum services using an enterprise service bus, in: International Conference on Product-Focused Software Process Improvement, Springer, 2023, pp. 107–118. doi:10.1007/978-3-031-49269-3_11.

[60]   V. Yussupov, U. Breitenbücher, C. Krieger, F. Leymann, J. Soldani, M. Wurster, Pattern-based modelling, integration, and deployment of microservice architectures, in: 2020 IEEE 24th International Enterprise Distributed Object Computing Conference (EDOC), IEEE, 2020, pp. 40–50. doi:10.1109/EDOC49727.2020.00015.

[61]   A. Ahmad, A. B. Altamimi, J. Aqib, A reference architecture for quantum computing as a service, arXiv preprint arXiv:2306.04578 (2023). doi:10.48550/arXiv.2306.04578.

[62]   M. P. Papazoglou, Service-oriented computing: Concepts, characteristics and directions, in: Proceedings of the Fourth International Conference on Web Information Systems Engineering, 2003. WISE 2003., IEEE, 2003, pp. 3–12. doi:10.1109/WISE.2003.1254461.

[63]   M. Endrei, J. Ang, A. Arsanjani, S. Chua, P. Comte, P. Krogdahl, M. Luo, T. Newling, Patterns: service-oriented architecture and web services, IBM Corporation, International Technical Support Organization New York, NY â, 2004.

[64]   S. G. Haugeland, P. H. Nguyen, H. Song, F. Chauvel, Migrating monoliths to microservices-based customizable multi-tenant cloud-native apps, in: 2021 47th Euromicro Conference on Software Engineering and Advanced Applications (SEAA), IEEE, 2021, pp. 170–177. doi:10.1109/SEAA53835.2021.00030.

[65]   L. Wang, G. Von Laszewski, A. Younge, X. He, M. Kunze, J. Tao, C. Fu, Cloud computing: a perspective study, New generation computing 28 (2010) 137–146. doi:10.1007/s00354-008-0081-5.

[66]   C. Hooton, Examining the economic contributions of the cloud to the united states economy, Report. Internet Association. Washington, DC (2019). https://ssrn.com/abstract=3347696

[67]   R. Pérez-Castillo, M. Piattini, The quantum software engineering path., in: Q-SET@ QCE, 2020, pp. 1–4.

[68]   J. Barzen, F. Leymann, M. Falkenthal, D. Vietz, B. Weder, K. Wild, Relevance of near-term quantum computing in the cloud: A humanities perspective, in: International Conference on Cloud Computing and Services Science, Springer, 2020, pp. 25–58.   doi:10.1007/978-3-030-72369-9_2.

[69]   E. Moguel, J. Rojo, D. Valencia, J. Berrocal, J. Garcia-Alonso, J. M. Murillo, Quantum service-oriented computing: current landscape and challenges, Software Quality Journal 30 (4) (2022) 983–1002. doi:10.1007/s11219-022-09589-y.

[70]   C. Richardson, Microservices patterns: with examples in Java, Simon and Schuster, 2018.

[71]   E. Wolff, Microservices: A Practical Guide: Principles, Concepts, and Recipes, Manning, 2019.

[72]   A. Akbulut, H. G. Perros, Software versioning with microservices through the api gateway design pattern, in: 9th International Conference on Advanced Computer Information Technologies (ACIT), IEEE, 2019, pp. 289–292. doi:10.1109/ACITT.2019.8779952.

[73]   P. Dreher, M. Ramasami, Prototype container-based platform for extreme quantum computing algorithm development, in: High Performance Extreme Computing Conference (HPEC), IEEE, 2019, pp. 1–7. doi:10.1109/HPEC.2019.8916430.

[74]   I. Kumara, W.-J. Van Den Heuvel, D. A. Tamburri, Qsoc: Quantum service-oriented computing, in: Symposium and Summer School on Service-Oriented Computing, Springer, 2021, pp. 52–63. doi:10.1007/978-3-030-87568-8_3.

[75]   M. Grossi, L. Crippa, A. Aita, G. Bartoli, V. Sammarco, E. Picca, N. Said, F. Tramonto, F. Mattei, A serverless cloud integration for quantum computing, arXiv preprint (2021). doi:10.48550/arXiv.2107.02007.

[76]   J. S. Bell, On the einstein podolsky rosen paradox, Physics Physique Fizika 1 (1964).

[77]   S. Jiang, K. A. Britt, A. J. McCaskey, T. S. Humble, S. Kais, Quantum annealing for prime factorization, Scientific reports 8 (1) (2018) 17667. doi:10.1038/s41598-018-36058-z.

[78]   R. Haring, M. Ohmacht, T. Fox, M. Gschwind, D. Satterfield, K. Sugavanam, P. Coteus, P. Heidelberger, M. Blumrich, R. Wisniewski, et al., The ibm blue gene/q compute chip, Ieee Micro 32 (2) (2011) 48–60. doi:10.1109/MM.2011.108.

[79]   B. Wang, F. Hu, H. Yao, C. Wang, Prime factorization algorithm based on parameter optimization of ising model, Scientific reports 10 (1) (2020) 7106. doi:10.1038/s41598-020-62802-5.

[80]   M. Motta, C. Sun, A. T. Tan, M. J. OâRourke, E. Ye, A. J. Minnich, F. G. Brandao, G. K.-L. Chan, Determining eigenstates and thermal states on

a quantum computer using quantum imaginary time evolution, Nature Physics 16 (2) (2020) 205–210. doi:10.1038/s41567-019-0704-4.

[81] D. Kielpinski, C. Monroe, D. J. Wineland, Architecture for a large-scale ion-trap quantum computer, Nature 417 (6890) (2002) 709–711. doi:10.1038/nature00784.

[82] N. M. Edwin, Software frameworks, architectural and design patterns, Journal of Software Engineering and Applications (2014). doi:10.4236/jsea.2014.78061.

[83] A. A. Khan, A. Ahmad, M. Waseem, P. Liang, M. Fahmideh, T. Mikkonen, et al., Software architecture for quantum computing systems—a systematic review, Journal of Systems and Software 201 (2023). doi:10.1016/j.jss.2023.111682.

[84] J. Garcia, M. Mirakhorli, L. Xiao, Y. Zhao, I. Mujhid, K. Pham, A. Okutan, S. Malek, R. Kazman, Y. Cai, et al., Constructing a shared infrastructure for software architecture analysis and maintenance, in: 18th International Conference on Software Architecture (ICSA), IEEE, 2021, pp. 150–161. doi:10.1109/ICSA51549.2021.00022.

[85] N. Killoran, J. Izaac, N. Quesada, V. Bergholm, M. Amy, C. Weedbrook, Strawberry fields: A software platform for photonic quantum computing, Quantum 3 (2019) 129. doi:10.22331/q-2019-03-11-129.

[86] J. Garcia-Alonso, J. Rojo, D. Valencia, E. Moguel, J. Berrocal, J. M. Murillo, Quantum Software as a Service Through a Quantum API Gateway, IEEE Internet Computing 26 (1) (2022) 34–41. doi:10.1109/MIC.2021.3132688.

[87] J. Alvarado-Valiente, J. Romero-Álvarez, E. Moguel, J. García-Alonso, J. M. Murillo, Technological diversity of quantum computing providers: a comparative study and a proposal for api gateway integration, Software Quality Journal (2023) 1–21doi:10.1007/S11219-023-09633-5/FIGURES/5.

[88] S. Bhavya, A. S. Pillai, Prediction models in healthcare using deep learning, in: Advances in Intelligent Systems and Computing, Vol. 1182 AISC, Springer, 2019, pp. 195–204. doi:10.1007/978-3-030-49345-5_21.

[89] J. Romero-Álvarez, J. Alvarado-Valiente, E. Moguel, J. García-Alonso, J. M. Murillo, Leveraging api specifications for scaffolding quantum applications, in: 2023 IEEE International Conference on Quantum Computing and Engineering (QCE), Bellevue, Washington, USA, 2023, pp. 187–190.

[90] R. Pérez-Castillo, M. A. Serrano, M. Piattini, Software modernization to embrace quantum technology, Advances in Engineering Software 151 (2021) 102933. doi:10.1016/j.advengsoft.2020.102933.

[91]   J. Alvarado-Valiente, J. Romero-Álvarez, A. Díaz, M. Rodríguez, I. García-Rodríguez, E. Moguel, J. Garcia-Alonso, J. M. Murillo, Quantum services generation and deployment process: A quality-oriented approach, in: International Conference on the Quality of Information and Communications Technology, Springer, 2023, pp. 200–214. doi:10.1007/978-3-031-43703-8_15.

[92]   J. Romero-Álvarez, J. Alvarado-Valiente, E. Moguel, J. García-Alonso, J. M. Murillo, Using OpenAPI for the Development of Hybrid Classical-Quantum Services, in: International Conference on Service-Oriented Computing, Springer, 2022, pp. 364–368. doi:10.1007/978-3-031-26507-5_34.

[93]   M. Esbensen, P. Bjørn, Routine and standardization in global software development, in: Proceedings of the 2014 ACM International Conference on Supporting Group Work, 2014, pp. 12–23. doi:10.1145/2660398.2660413.

[94]   S. Valverde, The long and winding road: Accidents and tinkering in software standardization, Metode Science Studies Journal (2021) 91–97doi:10.7203/metode.11.16112.

[95]   A. Neumann, N. Laranjeiro, J. Bernardino, An analysis of public rest web service apis, IEEE Transactions on Services Computing 14 (4) (2018) 957–970. doi:10.1109/TSC.2018.2847344.

[96]   A. Furutanpey, J. Barzen, M. Bechtold, S. Dustdar, F. Leymann, P. Raith, F. Truger, Architectural vision for quantum computing in the edge-cloud continuum, in: 2023 IEEE International Conference on Quantum Software (QSW), IEEE Computer Society, Los Alamitos, CA, USA, 2023, pp. 88–103. doi:10.1109/QSW59989.2023.00021.

[97]   J. Romero-Alvarez, J. Alvarado-Valiente, E. Moguel, J. Garcia-Alonso, J. M. Murillo, A workflow for the continuous deployment of quantum services, in: 2023 IEEE International Conference on Software Services Engineering (SSE), IEEE, 2023, pp. 1–8. doi:10.1109/SSE60056.2023.00015.

[98]   J. Romero-Álvarez, J. Alvarado-Valiente, E. Moguel, J. Garcia-Alonso, Quantum web services: Development and deployment, in: International Conference on Web Engineering, Springer, 2023, pp. 421–423. doi:10.1007/978-3-031-34444-2_39.

[99]   L. Leite, C. Rocha, F. Kon, D. Milojicic, P. Meirelles, A survey of devops concepts and challenges, ACM Computing Surveys (CSUR) 52 (6) (2019). doi:10.1145/3359981.

[100]   J. Alvarado-Valiente, J. Romero-Álvarez, E. Moguel, J. García-Alonso, Quantum web services orchestration and management using devops techniques, in: International Conference on Web Engineering, 2023, pp. 389–394. doi:10.1007/978-3-031-34444-2_33.

[101] J. Kelly, R. Barends, A. G. Fowler, A. Megrant, E. Jeffrey, T. C. White, D. Sank, J. Y. Mutus, et al., State preservation by repetitive error detection in a superconducting quantum circuit, Nature 519 (2015) 66–69. doi:10.1038/nature14270.

[102] I.-D. Gheorghe-Pop, N. Tcholtchev, T. Ritter, M. Hauswirth, Quantum devops: towards reliable and applicable nisq quantum computing, in: 2020 IEEE Globecom Workshops (GC Wkshps, IEEE, 2020, pp. 1–6. doi:10.1109/GCWkshps50303.2020.9367411.

[103] B. Weder, J. Barzen, F. Leymann, D. Vietz, Quantum software development lifecycle, in: Quantum Software Engineering, Springer, 2022, pp. 61–83. doi:0.1007/978-3-031-05324-5_4.

[104] M. Shahin, M. A. Babar, L. Zhu, Continuous integration, delivery and deployment: a systematic review on approaches, tools, challenges and practices, IEEE access 5 (2017) 3909–3943. doi:10.1109/ACCESS.2017.2685629.

[105] H. T. Nguyen, M. Usman, R. Buyya, Qfaas: A serverless function-as-a-service framework for quantum computing, arXiv preprint arXiv:2205.14845 (2022). doi:10.48550/arXiv.2205.14845.

[106] D. A. Lidar, H. Wang, Calculating the thermal rate constant with exponential speedup on a quantum computer, Physical Review E 59 (2) (1999) 2429. doi:10.1103/PhysRevE.59.2429.

[107] M. Martonosi, M. Roetteler, Next steps in quantum computing: Computer science's role, arXiv preprint arXiv:1903.10541 (2019). doi:10.48550/arXiv.1903.10541.

[108] R. Wille, R. Drechsler, Formal methods for em erging technologies, in: IEEE/ACM International Conference on Computer-Aided Design (ICCAD), IEEE, 2015, pp. 65–70. doi:10.1109/ICCAD.2015.7372551.

[109] B. Sodhi, Quality attributes on quantum computing platforms, arXiv preprint arXiv:1803.07407 (2018). doi:10.48550/arXiv.1803.07407.

[110] A. Bertolino, Software testing research: Achievements, challenges, dreams, in: Future of Software Engineering (FOSE'07), IEEE, 2007, pp. 85–103. doi:10.1109/FOSE.2007.25.

[111] M. Ying, Toward automatic verification of quantum programs, Formal Aspects of Computing 31 (1) (2019) 3–25. doi:10.1007/s00165-018-0465-3.

[112] M. Piattini, M. Serrano, R. Perez-Castillo, G. Petersen, J. L. Hevia, Toward a quantum software engineering, IT Professional 23 (1) (2021) 62–66. doi:10.1109/MITP.2020.3019522.

[113] A. Miranskyy, L. Zhang, On testing quantum programs, in: IEEE/ACM 41st International Conference on Software Engineering: New Ideas and Emerging Results (ICSE-NIER), IEEE, 2019, pp. 57–60. doi:10.1109/ICSE-NIER.2019.00023.

[114] A. García de la Barrera, García-Rodríguez de Guzmán,, M. Polo, M. Piattini, Quantum software testing: State of the art, Journal of Software: Evolution and Process (2021). doi:10.1002/smr.2419.

[115] S. Krishnaswamy, I. L. Markov, J. P. Hayes, Tracking uncertainty with probabilistic logic circuit testing, IEEE Design & Test of Computers 24 (4) (2007) 312–321. doi:10.1109/MDT.2007.146.

[116] C. A. R. Hoare, An axiomatic basis for computer programming, Communications of the ACM 12 (10) (1969) 576–580. doi:10.1145/363235.363259.

[117] G. Barthe, J. Hsu, M. Ying, N. Yu, L. Zhou, Relational proofs for quantum programs, arXiv preprint arXiv:1901.05184 (2019). doi:10.1145/3371089.

[118] L. Zhou, N. Yu, M. Ying, An applied quantum hoare logic, in: Proceedings of the 40th ACM SIGPLAN Conference on Programming Language Design and Implementation, 2019, pp. 1149–1162. doi:10.1145/3314221.3314584.

[119] E. Fredkin, T. Toffoli, Conservative logic, International Journal of theoretical physics 21 (3) (1982) 219–253. doi:10.1007/BF01857727.

[120] K. N. Patel, J. P. Hayes, I. L. Markov, Fault testing for reversible circuits, IEEE Transactions on Computer-Aided Design of Integrated Circuits and Systems 23 (8) (2004) 1220–1230. doi:10.1109/TCAD.2004.831576.

[121] ISO, Iso/iec 25010, Systems and software engineering - Systems and software Quality Requirements and Evaluation (SQuaRE) - Guide to SQuaRE. Retrieved from Systems and software engineering - Systems and software Quality Requirements and Evaluation (SQuaRE) - System and software quality models (2011).

[122] ISO, Iso/iec 25000, Systems and software engineering – Systems and software Quality Requirements and Evaluation (SQuaRE) – Guide to SQuaRE (2014).

[123] M. Rodríguez, M. Piattini, Software product quality evaluation using iso/iec 25000, ERCIM News 99 (2014).

[124] N. Moll, P. Barkoutsos, S. Benjamin, Quantum development beyond qiskit, npj Quantum Information 7 (1) (2021) 1–7.

[125] A. Khan, M. Akbar, A. Ahmad, M. Fahmideh, M. Shameem, V. Lahtinen, M. Waseem, T. Mikkonen, 2023 IEEE International Conference on Quantum Software (QSW), IEEE, 2023, Ch. Agile Practices for Quantum Software Development: Practitioners' Perspectives, pp. 9–20. doi:10.1109/QSW59989.2023.00012.

[126] M. Rodríguez, M. Piattini, C. Fernández, A hard look at software quality: Pilot program uses iso/iec 25000 family to evaluate, improve and certify software products, Quality Progress 48 (9) (2015) 30–36.

[127] J. Verdugo, J. Oviedo, M. Rodríguez, M. Piattini, Connecting research and practice for software product quality certification: a 25-year journey, Accepted to IEEE Software (2024). doi:10.1109/MS.2024.3357119.

[128] A. Kumar, Formalization of structural test cases coverage criteria for quantum software testing, International Journal of Theoretical Physics 62 (2023) 1–16. doi:10.1007/s10773-022-05271-y.

[129] M. Rodríguez, J. R. Oviedo, M. Piattini, Evaluation of software product functional suitability: A case study, Software Quality Professional 18 (3) (2016) 18. URL https://api.semanticscholar.org/CorpusID:114609549

[130] A. Cobb, J.-G. Schneider, K. Lee, Towards Higher-Level Abstractions for Quantum Computing, Association for Computing Machinery (ACM), 2022, pp. 115–124. doi:10.1145/3511616.3513106.

[131] I. Iso, iec/ieee international standard-systems and software engineering-vocabulary, ISO/IEC/IEEE 24765: 2017 (E) (2017).

[132] A. García de la Barrera, Agbamo/qtcc: Automatic testing for application-level deterministic quantum circuits by the use of an artifact called quantum test case circuit. (2023). doi:10.2139/ssrn.4421955.

[133] J. Cruz-Lemus, L. Marcelo, M. Piattinid, Towards a set of metrics for quantum circuits understandability, International Conference on the Quality of Information and Communications Technology (QUATIC 2021) (2021) 233–249. doi:10.1007/978-3-030-85347-1_18.

[134] A. Díaz, M. Rodríguez, M. Piattini, Towards a set of metrics for hybrid (quantum/classical) systems maintainability, Journal of Universal Computer Science (J.UCS) 30 (1) (2024) 25–48. doi:10.3897/jucs.99348.

[135] P. Shor, Algorithms for quantum computation: discrete logarithms and factoring, Proceedings 35th Annual Symposium on Foundations of Computer Science (1994) 124–134doi:10.1109/SFCS.1994.365700.

Index